Whispering to your Heart

Comforting Poetry in Seasons of Grief

Whispering to your Heart

Comforting Poetry in Seasons of Grief

Written by
Hazel Prosser

Edited by
AnnMarie Reynolds

Copyright © 2024 by Hazel Prosser

All rights reserved.

No portion of this book may be reproduced in any form without written permission from the publisher or author, except as permitted by UK copyright law.

This publication is designed to provide accurate and authoritative information in regard to the subject matter covered. It is sold with the understanding that neither the author nor the publisher is engaged in rendering legal, investment, accounting or other professional services. While the publisher and author have used their best efforts in preparing this book, they make no representations or warranties with respect to the accuracy or completeness of the contents of this book and specifically disclaim any implied warranties of merchantability or fitness for a particular purpose. No warranty may be created or extended by sales representatives or written sales materials. The advice and strategies contained herein may not be suitable for your situation. You should consult with a professional when appropriate. Neither the publisher nor the author shall be liable for any loss of profit or any other commercial damages, including but not limited to special, incidental, consequential, personal, or other damages.

First paperback edition published in the UK in August 2024

Book Cover by AnnMarie Reynolds (some use of AI generated images)

Portrait Photography © Sarah Baldock 2024 (www.sarahbaldockportraits.co.uk)

Snapshot and Family Photography © Hazel Prosser

ISBN 978-1-915353-26-9 (paperback)
ISBN 978-1-915353-27-6 (ebook)

Published by *begin a book* Independent Publishers

www.beginabook.com

To George and Hugo,

The sunshine through life's showers

and the rainbow in my heart.

ACKNOWLEDGEMENTS

Grief is a complex emotion that can hit us hard, whether it's triggered by the loss of a pet or a person. The depth of our sorrow reflects the love we shared with those we've lost and I believe that it's impossible to compare grief experiences, because each loss is deeply personal and impactful in its own way.

I have often mourned pets more intensely than people, simply because their loyalty, companionship, and unconditional love have been unmatched. Constant companions through thick and thin, they've neither judged nor complained. Yet, there are also individuals in my life who have shown me exceptional kindness and support, given me the courage to carry on, the hope to hold onto and the motivation to push forward. Words of gratitude don't feel sufficient, but I'm going to give it my best shot by using these couple of pages in this, my first book, to acknowledge them.

Firstly, to my parents, Bill and Heather Prosser who not only gave me life, but shaped me into the person I am today. I will forever be grateful for everything they did, how hard they worked in often difficult times and the lessons I have learned from simply being their daughter. I only wish I had expressed my gratitude more freely when I had the chance. May the grace of God bless you both and keep you safe until we are reunited in everlasting glory.

Dad ~ thank you for teaching me how to read, write and spell before I even started school. My love of words began with you as you patiently explained the origins of words, phrases and even street names. Together we enjoyed your passion for history and I have nothing but fond memories of the hours we spent browsing antique shops, whilst you told me everything you knew about a certain item. I absorbed every word, easily imagining myself living in a time gone by. In March 2003, your time on this earth came to a devastating end and through my grief I remember promising you one thing. "One day, I'll make you proud of me," I said. I hope that by writing this book, I have kept that unforgotten promise.

Mum ~ it feels like an eternity since you left me, though in reality is has been but a short while. I miss you more than I can ever express. You were the most practical, hard-working, creative and compassionate person and though your own life wasn't easy, you were always ready with a helping hand for others. My love for animals comes from you, your knowledge and passion perhaps your most precious gift to me. "Animals," you would say, "never disappoint us and we always know where we stand." How right you were. With skilled hands you created intricate tapestries, decorated houses and transformed gardens; there was nothing you couldn't do. The last words I said to you remain true to this day. I'm so proud of you, mum and I always will be, but more importantly I am so proud that I got to call you my mum.

My thanks extend now to those who have believed in me, encouraged me and guided me on this journey to becoming an author. It was a dream, something I never truly saw happening, yet with their support, I am here, writing their names on my very own Acknowledgements page. It is as surreal as it is beautiful.

To Guy & Gill Worrall, Kenda Summers, Sharon Gregory & Andrea Kenney ~

You've always encouraged me to have faith in my skills and potential. It can be tough to accept what others see in you when you can't see it yourself but thank you so much for your support through life's toughest obstacles.

To AnnMarie Reynolds ~

A great Editor is essential for every good book and though this journey was unexpected, with your professional expertise, patience and advice I now feel proud of what I have accomplished. Because of you, I can finally call myself an author.

To my Cherished Fur-and-Fin Family Members ~

Who have, since the moment of my arrival into this world, blessed my life. Through my writing, I pay tribute to you and preserve your memory. Our bond remains unbreakable, and though you may no longer be physically present, you will forever occupy a special place in my heart.

And last, but definitely not least, to Henry and Heidi ~

My two wonderful cats who are carrying on in the paw-steps of those who went before them. You are my very special family.

CONTENTS

HOW TO READ THIS BOOK — 11

SECTION ONE - POETRY FOR PET LOSS — 13
WHISPERING TO YOUR HEART — 15
BLESSED WITH THE BEST — 21
PERPETUAL FRIENDSHIP — 25
A PET'S PLEA ... — 29
A YEAR WITH YOU — 33
ALONE INSIDE MY HEAD — 37
DEAFENING SILENCE — 41
SIGNS FROM ME — 45
THE LAMENT — 49
WANDERING DOWN MEMORY LANE — 53
LEAVING HOME — 59
LOVE IN ASHES — 63
THE FINAL GOODBYE — 67
EMOTIONAL CONFETTI — 71
HOUSEWORK DAY — 75
WINTER WANDERING ... & WONDERING — 79

SECTION TWO - POETRY FOR HOLIDAYS & ANNIVERSARIES — 83
ANNIVERSARIES — 85
THE ETERNAL CHRISTMAS CARD — 89
THE PRICELESS GIFT — 93
WE ARE ONE - NEW YEAR MESSAGE — 97
WILL YOU SAVE ME A PLACE THIS CHRISTMAS? — 101
ON THE CUSP OF TOMORROW ~ ANTICIPATORY GRIEF ~ — 105

SECTION THREE - POETRY FOR FAMILY — 111
TIME MOVES ON - THE FIRST MONTH — 113
A LIFE FOREVER CHANGED — 117

LISTEN TO YOUR HEART	121
LUCKY SIXPENCE	123
THE EMOTIONAL CAROUSEL	127
THE FIRST ANNIVERSARY	131
LIVE EVERY DAY AS IF IT WERE YOUR LAST	135
MY FINAL WISH	139

SECTION FOUR - POETRY FOR (ALL) TIMES OF GRIEF — 143

BONDED	145
TALK TO ME - LET MY NAME LIVE ON	149
THE HEAVENLY CANDLE	153
UNIQUE AND PRECIOUS TIMES	157
DEAR GRIEF … YOU WILL NOT WIN!	161
I KNOW YOU CAN STILL HEAR ME	165
NATURE'S INVITATION	169
THE FEATHER IN THE WOODS	173
CANDLELIGHT REFLECTIONS	177
LITTLE ROBIN	181
MOON GAZING HARE	183

SECTION FIVE - POETRY FOR FRIENDS AND EMPLOYERS — 187

GROUNDING THOUGHTS	189
THE GRIEVING EMPLOYEE	193
DEAR FRIEND, DON'T FORSAKE ME NOW	197

SECTION SIX - BESPOKE POETRY — 201

DEAR SKYE	203
CHOSEN	207
ABOUT THE AUTHOR	213

SECTION SEVEN - HELPFUL RESOURCES — 215

THE WHISPERING JOURNAL - A PLACE FOR MY THOUGHTS	219

Praise for the author ...

"Hazel's writing is a lifeline for those drowning in grief, wrapping them in a warm embrace of understanding and compassion. Her heartfelt words resonate deeply, offering a glimmer of hope in the darkest times. Through her stories & poems, the bereaved find a safe haven where their pain is acknowledged and their journey is gently supported."

Jacqui Gunn

"Hazel seems to have previously hidden her light under a bushel. Who knew the depths of her quiet talent. Her debut book consisting of a series of poems are heartfelt and beautifully written. Reading her work leaves you mesmerised and she has a supreme ability to convey bittersweet sorrow which deeply stirs one's emotions. I highly recommend reading her work. This author is not done. This is just the beginning."

Sharon Gregory

"Hazel's poetry provides solace to those mourning the loss of a pet or loved one. As a Grief Counsellor, I deeply appreciate how her work resonates with readers and underscores the importance of addressing grief openly through poetry. Her words serve as comfort food for the broken soul."

Kenda Summers

How to read this book ...

When you open the pages, you'll see I've included a brief overview to accompany each poem. These I've written for two reasons: firstly, so that you can identify with my thoughts and feelings at the time of their creation and secondly, to help you choose which poems will give you the most comfort and support.

The book is also divided into sections to make it easier to navigate. Whilst I began writing poetry to help me come to terms with the devastating loss of my own pets over the years, it became apparent as I began to collate these poems, that many could relate to any loss or circumstance of grief. The sections are therefore broad and for guidance only. Any poem within this book will, I hope, bring you comfort.

One thing I really wanted to achieve was a feeling of unity. Often, I have found grief to be misunderstood and even sidelined, especially when it comes to the loss of our pets. This is not okay. We all grieve differently and I wanted you as the reader to be able to have a feeling of belonging, a feeling of not being alone, which is why each poem has its own little backstory. You may read through one particular overview and find yourself nodding along because you've felt that way too. You will be reassured that you are not alone, even if your comfort is coming from the words of someone you've never met.

You can also skip past each overview if you prefer, and read the poems on their own - whatever feels right for you. This book is here to help you, wherever you are in your journey; there is no right or wrong way to travel the road of grief. Take all that you need from these pages, give yourself time to pause and reflect and above all, allow yourself to grieve.

At the end of the book I have listed some useful resources and groups that you may wish to explore.

Thinking of each of you, Hazel x

SECTION ONE

Poetry for
PET LOSS

WHISPERING TO YOUR HEART

There was only ever going to be one poem opening my debut poetry collection, and it is this same poem which also lends its name to the compendium's title. Prior to even conceiving the possibility of writing a book, I had received encouragement from many who'd found solace in the words of 'Whispering to your Heart', which was written during the heartbreaking loss of my handsome cat, Hugo. The realisation that my words, written through floods of tears, could impact so many people was humbling and I know today that without their encouragement, I would never have put this book together.

It was in the early hours of 6th July 2020, in the throes of a pandemic, when I woke to find that Hugo, had passed away in his sleep. There had been no warning, so both the shock and grief were overwhelming. It was a tragic reminder of how quickly life can change and how loved ones can leave us in a moment, a second almost, at a time when we are least expecting it.

The losses I have experienced throughout my life have been so incredibly difficult to bear and I always find night-times the worst. This is when pain is amplified by the stillness and silence of the darkness and all I can hear are the thunderous emotions which are echoing through my empty heart.

After Hugo passed away, I would often find myself wandering aimlessly around the house, particularly at night when it was almost impossible to sleep. Henry and Heidi, my other two cats, were trying their best to comfort me, but they too were feeling Hugo's loss keenly. Henry especially began to pine terribly, even refusing to eat, to the point I was convinced I would lose him, too.

During this time, though, I began to see clearly the incredible qualities animals possess. Heidi 'stepped up' for both Henry and I, never leaving either of our sides, her constant presence reassuring and calming. I know that she was taking care of us in her own feline way and without Heidi, I do think Henry would have struggled even more than he did. When he withdrew, Heidi would be persistent in encouring him to play, reminding him that we were all in this together and slowly he pulled through. As I watched their beautiful interaction in a time of such devastating grief, it was proof - if any were needed - that animals do understand human emotions, perhaps even better than we do ourselves.

During one of my night-time wanders through the house, I decided to turn on my computer and type whatever I needed, onto a blank screen. My head was so full of emotion I was unable to articulate and suddenly it made sense to allow my fingers the freedom to roam across the keyboard without any conscious thought.

Eventually, overcome with tiredness, I stopped typing and sat back, allowing a moment of peace, and it was then that I began to hear words. A poem forming inside my head. Instinctively I felt as though Hugo was communicating with me, letting me know he was okay. He had been a gentle soul, calm, never fazed, a big teddy bear of a cat, and in that bleak, early morning haze I knew he was with me, beside me, just as if he had never left. Blinking his gorgeous sky-blue eyes at me one more time.

Without conscious thought I deleted everything on the page and started again, only this time I captured the words that were forming in my head, floating to me as if from another world. Though I cried as I typed every single one, I knew I was experiencing something incredibly special.

As always, Henry and Heidi were right with me and once I had finished, I looked to where they slept, my heart bursting with love - and then it hit me.

We were a true family, the three of us, and Hugo had been a massive part of that, too.

Families come in all shapes and sizes and my family, that night, finally began to know peace.

Through 'Whispering To Your Heart', Hugo was telling us not to be so desolate, that he was okay and that by giving us this message, his precious gift, the three of us began to heal.

When I see others experiencing their own precious gift through the words of this poem, I feel my connection to Hugo once more. As if he is beside me, alongside me, my hand holding his paw.

Though nothing will ever take away the pain of his passing, 'Whispering to your Heart' is Hugo's legacy - a legacy which will continue to bring his special kind of love to all it touches.

WHISPERING TO YOUR HEART

*Time to sleep,
To rest your head
The day is done,
Enough's been said*

*Before you do,
I just ask this -
Talk to me,
Send me a kiss.*

*That closing thought,
The wandering tear,
I promise you,
I am still here.*

*What you cannot see,
Yet feel so strong,
Our inseparable spirits,
Guiding you along.*

*Watching from afar,
As your eyes close tight,
Then curling next to you,
As with every night.*

Hush your thoughts,
I'll comfort you,
Warming your soul,
Guiding you through.

Feel the weight,
Lift from your mind,
Our love's eternal,
Hearts entwined.

So sleep for now,
Relax, unwind.
And as you dream,
In time you'll find.

I've left a gift,
This much is true,
You are me ...
And, I am you.

© Hazel Prosser 2020

BLESSED WITH THE BEST

I have a deep fondness for this poem because, in the midst of my sadness, I tried to imagine the perspective of the beloved animals who have passed away. Even though I wrote these words shortly after Hugo's departure, I feel they represent all the animals I have loved.

Animals spend their whole lives delighting us, pleasing us, providing everlasting companionship and friendship. I personally do not believe that this ends once they are out of sight, which I allude to in the first verse.

The second verse references destiny and how, out of the millions of animals in this world, our special one chose us.

Verse three describes the initial and lifelong connection between human and animal. I don't think I've met a devoted pet parent yet who, once meeting their 'new baby' for the first time, hasn't felt excited about what the future holds as their friendship develops.

Animals live their lives beautifully free of complication. They don't have the stresses we do, no bills to pay, no job to answer to, no routine to dictate what they can and cannot do, so they concentrate on what is relevant to them, and aren't they all the better for it? I think so!

Moving on to verse five, a purring cat on one's lap, a loyal dog by one's side, or a horse to show you the freedom of the wider world, no matter what the animal is. From the smallest hamster to the largest horse, they are unencumbered. They become our best friends, best counsellors and perhaps ultimately, the best of us.

The penultimate verse really links in with the third. As much as we don't like to think about it, the reality is that we are likely to outlive our animal companion and we know they will end up breaking our hearts. When I first collected Hugo from his breeder, I looked into his beautiful blue eyes and whispered, *"You are so perfect, I'm so lucky to have found you, yet one day Hewg, one day, you're going to break my heart wide open."*

My little boy blinked right back at me and in that moment, I knew that before he ever broke my heart, we would enjoy the most special and irreplaceable of times.

There are never enough words to illustrate just how much the friendship of our animals means to us. It's like an enchanted secret.

But we know and that's enough. It is as it should be.

BLESSED WITH THE BEST

Please don't let my passing change you,
By the pain locked tight inside your chest,
What you simply never quite realised,
Is that you were chosen from all the rest.

Long before I knew I'd be yours,
Angels saw how much you cared,
They knew there was more love within you,
Which they decanted, and you shared.

The moment our eyes met each other,
Opening windows between your soul and mine,
A thread that would bond us eternally,
Was transposed like invisible twine.

I showed you how to live each day freely,
Not to be burdened by routine and chores,
How to ignore what didn't concern you,
And concentrate solely on that which was yours.

Humans are so wrapped up in worry,
Mostly situations not of their choice,
My job was to show you alternatives,
Through calmness, serenity and poise.

On earth we were lent to each other,
A friendship no words can accurately narrate,
Two souls enriched by life's tapestry,
United by the guiding hand of fate.

I need you to hear my words,
From where I eternally rest,
Because they're spoken with the truth I lived by,
When I say I was blessed with the best!

© Hazel Prosser 2022

PERPETUAL FRIENDSHIP

'Perpetual Friendship' - chosen deliberately (as opposed to 'eternal') due to the presence of the word 'pet' in the centre of 'perpetual.'

In this poem, let's envisage a world where our beloved animals now dwell. So beautiful, so pure, so perfect in every way.

Anyone who has ever been blessed with an animal knows that their loyalty never falters. From a world unseen, our animals are still watching over us, listening to us, hearing us, guiding us and loving us.

Within their new world, they have made friends. One day, one of them, taking a momentary break from eternal rest, decides to have a peek at the world they have left and see how their best human friend is doing. Upon seeing their pet parent profoundly grieving, they galvanise themselves into action to provide words of comfort. As in life, there's always one who has 'ideas,' so signs are sent to show they are contented and settled.

As I typed this poem, I had a Robin come right up to my door, a sign often considered to indicate the presence of a loved one – whether pet or human – who has passed on.

I hope this poem will provide comfort and reassurance, just like that little Robin gave me during that timely moment.

PERPETUAL FRIENDSHIP

Now settled into their new home,
Inquisitive pets say, "Let's see;
How the one we love so much
Is coping without you and me."

Looking down on the world they left,
With pride they mention you.
"I had the best throughout my life," (one says)
In unison, others nod, "Yes, and we did too!".

"See the one who thinks we've left,
Tears streaming down their face?
In time, the love and joy we shared together,
Will fill our empty place."

"What can we do?" (They discuss together).
"To show we'll never part."
"I know" says your beloved friend.
"We'll live on in their heart."

The cacophony of animal voices
In excitement do exclaim,
"This is only a temporary hiatus,
Because one day we'll meet again!"

What can we do to comfort them?
To bridge the passage of time?
I know! One pet asserts
"Let's send a frequent sign."

Now, when you look at the empty chair,
Or the little blanket on the ground.
Your beloved friend is showing you,
They are contented, safe and sound.

© Hazel Prosser 2023

A PET'S PLEA ...
(to their Grieving Owner)

This poem was written when my grief at the loss of my 'boys' (my beloved cats) was at its most and all-consuming. I wanted to allow them to 'speak' to me, to tell their story, to reassure me and above all, to comfort me.

I allowed these words to flow as I imagined them telling me how to live my life and encouraging me to be free of society's burdens and expectations.

In my experience, animals don't like seeing their owners upset and distressed; mine certainly didn't, which tells me that, in the same way we believe (as pet parents) that we have the 'best' pet, our pets also believe they have the 'best' pet parent.

What a lovely way to remember them and to provide comfort to us at the same time!

I hope you are able to relate to the words of this poem, as you adjust to life without your best friend, and bring you comfort knowing how special the time you shared was.

A PET'S PLEA ...
(to their Grieving Owner)

From my new home in paradise found,
I'm looking down on you.
I'm puzzled by your grief and think,
I need a word or two!

Your face is stained with tears,
Your heart and soul are torn.
You loved me more than life itself,
From the day that I was born.

You think there's more you could've done,
Please know this isn't true.
My time on earth was purely lent,
I'm so glad it was with you.

My early years were full of fun,
A ball of mischief wrapped in fur,
My antics made you laugh out loud!
I was the comedic connoisseur!

As the years rolled by, we became a team,
We lived life's ups and downs!
Some days were really very good,
Others brought unwanted frowns.

I knew when you required my paw,
To be wrapped around your wrist.
It was my way of saying you're not alone,
And I know you got the gist!

You often told me how you wished,
You saw life through my eyes.
I showed you how to take each day,
As a treasured new surprise.

I know how much you loved me,
I know you love me still.
In turn I loved you just as much,
And I always will!

You say you would do anything,
Absolutely anything for me!
So please take your tears and dry them,
I want you to be free!

That's free from guilt and anger,
Lose the sorrow and regret,
Live your live as I lived mine
From sunrise 'til sunset!

I want to see you happy!
Not dwelling on the past.
Embrace each day as it unfolds,
Because life goes by so fast.

I just have one more thing to say,
From my celestial rest.
From the tip of my tail to my whiskered face
I had the very best!

© Hazel Prosser 2022

A YEAR WITH YOU

I wrote this poem to describe a perfect, typical year with my beloved animals. It is essentially an overview of how each month unfolds and a thank you to the companions who never complain, never betray and are always steadfastly loyal.

I love the positive outlook of this poem and hope you can relate to it too!

A YEAR WITH YOU

January chills, snow and rain,
Creamy hot chocolate fills my mug,
You are there, curled up by my side,
Purring deeply, nice and snug.

February brings much the same,
Though hints of Spring sneak through,
You're either on my lap or at my feet.
The closing of Winter just with you.

March "roars in like a lion ...", people say,
It's time to Spring clean our home,
Whilst I'm busy with every household chore,
You ensure I'm never alone.

April dawns with fresh new life
Days graciously smile once more,
Brighter mornings, lighter nights
Back to gardening - with your helping paw!

May arrives, the maypole month,
Shaking hands with Summer's glow,
The garden, the trees, it's all so pretty,
Eyes sparkle, radiating the love you show.

June warmly takes us into Midsummer,
You frolic in the sun,
Chasing birds, butterflies, bees and ants,
Living your best life until the day is done.

July arrives with the hottest days,
Temperatures soaring high,
The bluest skies peppered with cotton wool clouds,
The sunniest spot you find to occupy!

August sees fields being harvested,
Wheat, barley, corn and rye.
We enjoy balmy days and burnished nights,
Underneath a cloudless bright blue sky.

September sees children back at school,
Summer holidays are now in the past,
Autumn's glow begins to show on the trees,
Life is going by so fast.

October, the month of Halloween
Clocks going back, nights drawing in.
You're sleeping more, with lessening light,
On the cusp of Winter, that will soon begin.

November's fireworks are not for you,
As bangs, shrieks and colours alight the sky,
You look at me, all questioning,
Not knowing the reason why.

December, the month of Christmas,
One of fun, celebration and cheer.
Thank you my little one, for the 12 months we've shared.
And here's to our Happy New Year!

© Hazel Prosser 2023

ALONE INSIDE MY HEAD

Losing an animal can be the most painful and isolating time in the life of the pet parent. Society can trivialise their passing, with many often underestimating the level of grief felt.

What is not always appreciated, is just how painful words of 'comfort' or 'consolation' can be to someone who is grieving the loss of their pet. If a person feels their grief being minimised (whether unintentionally or not) it can be isolating and cause damaging emotions to be repressed. Some of the 'least' helpful comments I have heard over the years are:

"Oh, I'm sorry to hear this. How old was he/she?"

"Oh, I didn't know he/she was sick. Are you okay?"

"I'm sorry, will you get another one?"

"Well, they were a good age for a cat/dog etc".

"When you're ready, there are plenty of animals in rescue centres".

"That's why I'll never have another animal, the pain is too much!"

"Remember the good times, that's what they'd want".

Though some of these are offered in kind, responding to the comforter with the suggestion that your grief may take a while to overcome, can, in my experience, be considered dramatic, over-emotional or even pathetic. I know because I have had each and every one of those comments directed at me.

If society could see inside the head of the person grieving, they would see memories of years, sometimes a decade or more, of devoted love and friendship. They would see the joy and happiness that each animal brought into that person's life, and they would understand that a family member is no longer around. The very best thing ever said to me, was when I lost George:

> "*I have absolutely no words and no real idea what to say, but I'm here to say nothing and let you talk if it helps*".

It DID help. Whilst I didn't take that particular friend up on their invitation, the fact they had not consoled me with an everyday cliché, meant a lot.

This poem was written during some of my earliest days of grief, after I had been asked yet again, "*Will you get another?*"

To anyone who doesn't understand, this is impossible. One can never 'get another'. Time may bring a new life into our homes, but that new animal will have their own personality and will be unique in his or her own right. They will be another much loved pet, but they will never replace the one who has been lost.

The words in this poem are written as guidance to the outside world, to show how to treat someone who is grieving an animal.

They need time, space and respect to come to terms with their loss, and I hope that the message within 'Alone Inside My Head' can help to support you or someone you love.

ALONE INSIDE MY HEAD

Alone inside my head I wonder,
Surmising what I'm supposed to do.
But look up to the velvet sky above,
And speak aloud to you.

No-one truly understands,
The lingering pain that grips my heart.
Or has time to take me by the hand,
Yet grief is tearing me apart.

"Will you get another?"
Those words sting like garden nettle.
My inner voice screams and shouts,
Stoically I draw upon my mettle.

"There'll never be another."
One can't replicate unique!
In time perhaps a new friend will be sent
For now, hush the words you speak!"

Momentarily distracted by my thoughts,
Something catches my tear-filled eyes.
A shooting star pierces the quiet of night,
And takes me by surprise!

My little one, I know this to be fact,
My soul has conversed with yours.
And sent the most beautiful sign to me,
Guided by loving paws.

When all is said, and all is done,
Never can we part.
For when I am feeling at my lowest ebb,
Blessed memories, soothe my aching heart.

© Hazel Prosser 2020

DEAFENING SILENCE

How does one accurately convey deepest emotional pain to those who have never known the love of an animal?

It is quite impossible, because trying to explain to those who don't understand when you're grappling with heightened grief isn't easy, in fact it's exhausting.

Everyone deals with grief in a different way; for some having friends or families visiting to help occupy the griever's mind can be perfect, yet for others, it can be the last thing they need. The truth of the matter is that there isn't any one generic answer, because we are all unique and it is important to respect each person's individual wishes. If they say they want to be 'alone with their thoughts,' then take it that they really do want to be alone.

'Deafening Silence' was written as a way to illustrate the importance of a grieving owners feelings – and to allow them silence if that is their need.

Take it from me how difficult it is to return to an empty home, seeing and hearing triggers wherever you go. The silence really is deafening. If you want to support someone who is grieving, perhaps take a moment to imagine what that silence might be like and consider how you can best offer comfort.

> ... *Silence is a deafening sound;*
>
> *Any grieving owner hears ...*

DEAFENING SILENCE

Would you dare to question,
How hard a devoted owner grieves.
When a whiskered face is absent,
From society quite illiterate of the bereaved?

Silence is a deafening sound,
The grieving owner hears.
No faithful barks, meows or purrs,
To comfort their flowing tears.

What was once a happy home,
Cradles reminders of their faithful friend.
Years of loyalty and unconditional love,
From which they knew they could depend.

No understanding from the outside world,
And the expectation not to mourn.
Because after all ,"It was only just a pet,
And not something in human form!"

What is not comprehended,
Is that grief cannot be compartmentalised.
It's a real emotion born out of love,
When any adored family member dies.

Pets can be in a person's life,
A companion reliable and steadfast.
Sometimes for years longer,
Than marriages have been known to last!

In time the pet parent will remember,
With fondness and with pride.
That blessed loving little soul,
Who was a constant at their side.

So please, don't dilute the silence,
Grievers need an understanding compassionate tone.
For the life they once enjoyed so much,
Feels so isolated, and all alone.

© Hazel Prosser 2023

SIGNS FROM ME

I wrote this poem imagining one of my beloved cats speaking to me as I carried out my daily chores. They would be constantly assuring me of their presence and reminding me that they are by my side, offering unwavering love and support.

But rather than being able to see them here, though, they make their presence known by way of signs, signs from, their new world.

In the second verse I have used the word 'purring' which is specific to cats, however you can remove this verse completely if it is not appropriate. This poem then becomes one which can soothe for any loss.

SIGNS FROM ME

Let me reassure you,
I am here at your side.
Visiting the home I love so much,
Accompanying you with pride.

I pad around from room to room,
Purring softly as I go.
You look so heavy-hearted,
Because you miss me so.

I hear the silent words,
Conversing in your head.
I dry the invisible tears,
And kiss the ones you shed.

I know you feel my presence,
As you go about your day.
I see you stop and look around,
Thoughts in disarray.

The radio plays our favourite song,
Pensively you pause.
The lyrics hold deep meaning,
They are mine and they are yours.

As you look out of the window,
There's a feather blowing free.
Take solace in these little signs,
They are sent with love from me.

© Hazel Prosser 2022

THE LAMENT
(of a Grieving Pet Parent)

With this poem, similar to some of the others, I wanted to shed light on how upsetting clichés can be when you are grieving for a beloved pet. When I had finished writing, I shared it with a childhood friend who has never owned a pet. I wanted her feedback, given she had never been in the position of grieving such a loss. I was thrilled when she not only read it, but also thanked me for helping her to understand the emotions of pet parents and how devastating it can be when their furry friend passes away.

It was exactly the response I was hoping for. I want this poem to educate others about the real, valid and painful grief experienced by pet loss. I also want to help those struggling to vocalise their emotions following a loss, to find their voice within these words, too.

THE LAMENT *(of a Grieving Pet Parent)*

DON'T ask me what the matter is!
When tears pool in my eyes.
DON'T dismiss the faltered explanation,
Of the pain that I disguise.

DON'T look at me with pity,
Or use the "only" word!
Because even though you've listened …
I can tell you haven't heard.

DON'T question why I'm in such pain,
As I bite my inside cheek.
DON'T make excuses, why you must leave,
When I'm feeling so weak.

DON'T you see that I'm in turmoil?
(As tears begin to roll).
I've lost a family member,
Who was my very heart and soul.

DON'T say my loss isn't human,
As if that will make things right!
The love I mourn, meant more to me,
And my days all feel like nights.

'There's many DON'T's I ask of you,
Though plenty start with 'DO'.
DO please spare a little of your time,
To realise all I'm going through.

DO take notice, without judgement,
And hear each grieving word.
Stay silent if I ask you to,
I'm begging to be heard.

To you I may have lost a 'pet',
But for years they've been my friend.
Devotedly accepting me for who I am,
So, my grief I will defend.

DO understand pet owners mourn,
Their loved one who is gone.
Support, console and hug them tight ,
As you would for anyone.

DO you now see why I'm in such pain?
Consumed with such regret?
I'm grieving for a family member,
Who wasn't "just .. a .. pet!"

© Hazel Prosser 2022

WANDERING DOWN MEMORY LANE

'Wandering Down Memory Lane' was inspired by a dream I had about my cat, Hugo. In this dream, Hugo was living in a picturesque 'chocolate box' style cottage and when I arrived, I found him lounging in the cosy living room. Immediately I went and picked him up, sensing his weight and hearing his contented purr which warmed my heart.

With Hugo cuddled tightly against my chest, I began to leave, delighted to be taking him home, yet Hugo had other ideas. He resisted, making it known that he had no intention of leaving this cottage and this room. At first I was confused at his reluctance but then everything stilled and a sense of tranquillity settled over me. It was then that I realised I had no need for confusion or concern. Hugo was happy here in his new home and his desire to stay was the reassurance I needed.

The impact of this dream has stayed with me, so much so, that I transformed it into this poem, 'Wandering Down Memory Lane', allowing myself (and you) to envision a place of solace. A perfect dwelling. A home of calm, warmth and love.

And the address?

        Number 1, Memory Lane.

By closing our eyes, we can imagine a world where our pets and loved ones now contentedly reside. It's there if we look.

WANDERING DOWN MEMORY LANE

It's quiet now
I'll take a walk
To my favourite address
Where the spirits talk.

My heart is punching,
And the tears explode!
My footsteps echo towards
This private abode.

I stare transfixed, then ...
Left, centre and right,
My eyes embrace
What comes into sight!

A familiar face,
One, two, then three ...
Yet more than this,
Hasten to welcome me

My tears flow quicker!
My heart excites!
My spirit quivers!
Under a silvery light.

*There's just one home
In Memory Lane,
And it's so unique,
Words can't explain.*

*The door opens,
We step right through.
It's cosy and warm
Beautiful too.*

*Those familiar faces are
Here with me.
The room illuminated
With spiritual esprit.*

*I love it! The purrs, The meows
The barks galore!
I'm being guided by
Their loving paw.*

*In unspoken words
I'm shown with glee,
They haven't left
They're here, with me!*

*Memory Lane
Is my spiritual throng,
My loving friends
Eternally guide me along.*

*My head bows,
They ask, "Why so blue?
Heavy-hearted
I whisper, "I so miss you!"*

*"But we haven't left!
We're here now!
Look around,
Mop your glistening brow."*

*"Mama you look
So very sad,
We don't want this,
You're all we had."*

*I whisper softly
"I've let you down"
You taught me well
Broken, I frown.*

*"I make mistakes.
Avoid those who care,
Grief envelops my soul
And lays it bare."*

*In fear of being
Hurt much more,
I reach down
For a velvet paw.*

I'm all alone
My life is hollow
Where once you stood
And still, you follow.

"Oh no, now Mama!
Speak our name!
We hear your words,
From whence we came!"

"It's a bond you see,
A gift bestowed.
We don't leave
Just move down the road!"

So, if you are struggling,
With grief and pain,
Remember to take
A wander down Memory Lane!

© Hazel Prosser 2022

LEAVING HOME *(in Hugo's Words)*

From the time he was a young kitten, Hugo had an air of calm and wisdom, earning him the endearing nickname of 'The Thinker'. He never really acted in a 'kitten-like' manner, always seeming to observe and consider whilst displaying moments of incredible intelligence. When Henry joined our family, for example, Hugo welcomed him openly, no fighting or hissing, just a happy curiosity. He even independently opened the door of Henry's carrier, eager to meet his new friend.

Henry and Hugo's bond went on to become something extraordinary, and after Hugo's passing, I continue to feel his presence around both myself and Henry.

Hugo was an exceptional companion who consistently provided reassurance and love to all, so this poem, which I wrote on the day he passed, is from Hugo's perspective. These are the words I believe he was saying as our little family bade him farewell.

LEAVING HOME (in Hugo's Words)

I left our home this morning,
Taking my eternal walk,
I know it broke your heart in two,
So let us have this talk.

You chose me as a baby,
But in fact, this much is true,
For me to say, that you were chosen,
Before I came to you.

The angels looked down on the earth,
To find the perfect home,
And when my time came to be born,
They knew I'd never be alone.

You had the pick of litter,
And saw I was the only boy,
The angels guided your decision,
As they knew I'd bring you joy.

You gave me the very best in life,
My bed was warm and snug,
Never did a day go by,
Where I failed to get a hug.

We went through many years,
Enjoying life's rich tapestry,
Lots of laughs and happy times,
Where there was you, I'd also be.

I was sent to teach you many things,
Patience, loyalty and love,
But my time was sadly limited,
Before I returned to God above.

I'm sorry you had no warning,
That I would leave this night,
I wanted no pain or struggle,
But to quietly slip from sight.

You were sleeping oh-so soundly,
I gave you a head butt of love,
Before the angels cradled and carried me,
To the celestial world above.

Please mourn for me no more,
Do not carry the weight of blame,
No why's, wherefores' or what could I have done?
In your heart I'm an eternal flame.

So dry your eyes, I beg of you,
You've cried many oceans of tears,
Just smile, reflect and be so proud,
We shared such happy years.

© Hazel Prosser 2020

LOVE IN ASHES

The period between the loss of a pet and the collection of their ashes can be days, maybe even a couple of weeks and in my experience (when I lost Hugo), it was a time of complete 'nothingness'. I was overwhelmed with his loss but felt unable to fully grieve until I could lay him to rest.

During this time I spent hours on the internet, looking for advice, words of comfort, articles, poetry, anything that would help me through this time of limbo. Yet I came up blank. Struggling to understand my emotions, I finally collected Hugo's ashes and it was only then I realised what I needed to do. I needed to turn once more to writing and capture my experience of that awful gap in time when I was waiting ... just waiting ...

'Love in Ashes' became a poetic reflection of this period and eventually, with both Henry and Heidi at my side, I was able to find solace in laying Hugo's ashes to rest under a beautiful rosebush.

The nothingness, the emptiness, the feelings of uselessness are incredibly difficult to cope with so I hope that through my story and my poem, you too can find that time of waiting just a little bit more bearable.

Remember, love in ashes is eternal.

> *" ... loyalty, love and friendship,*
> *that will sustain eternally."*

LOVE IN ASHES

Today I received a call,
The dreaded one I'd been expecting.
A faceless voice simply said,
"His ashes are ready for collecting."

My heart it broke again,
Endless tears streamed down my cheeks.
A notable absence of folk to lean on,
To them, my loss has now been weeks.

A mere trifle of time in life,
Since I said "Godspeed" to you.
My four-legged companion, my best friend,
Who could not have been more true.

I somehow retained my dignity,
As your little casket was placed in my hand.
I'm not sure what I was expecting,
Perhaps, someone to understand?

As I carefully drove us both back home,
I spoke to you along the way.
Telling you once again how much you meant
And how you brightened every day!

When we arrived into our sanctuary
I sat your casket on my knee.
And kissed the polished engraved plaque,
Which bore your name so splendidly.

Summoning my strength, I cradled you.
Taking you into every single room.
Then into your favourite place of all,
Our glorious garden in full perfume.

Your final resting place all ready,
An area, you loved to help me tend.
A rose bush with the biggest blooms.
Perfectly entitled "A Faithful Friend"

Thank you from my heart and soul,
For the decade you gave to me.
The loyalty, love, and friendship
That will sustain eternally.

© Hazel Prosser 2020

THE FINAL GOODBYE

This poem was one of those I struggled to write as tears flowed readily with each word. The pain of saying goodbye to a beloved pet is immense, and worse still (in my experience), if you, as the pet parent, need to decide it's time to end their suffering.

In those moments of grief, making any sense of the situation can be impossible, so my intention with this poem is to capture the emotions of that final farewell - from the conflict of heart and mind to the acceptance of the inevitable.

From a pet's perspective, their narration is to offer reassurance and love to their human. To remind that person who has loved them unconditionally, that they have made the right choice. There is no need for guilt.

The end of the poem refers to the unbreakable bond which forms between human and pet, between lifelong friends and with affirmation again from the pet, that no matter how difficult this decision, it is their human's final act of enduring love.

> *"You lift your head and look around,*
>
> *A paw alights my knee.*
>
> *You give the biggest headbutt,*
>
> *You're wanting to be free."*

THE FINAL GOODBYE

Please tell me what am I to do?
My head is in a maelstrom.
I must accept the end is nigh,
And soon you will be gone.

You look at me with so much love,
Through soft and gentle eyes.
You seem to think I'm perfect,
When it's you who is so wise.

Guiding words are just white noise,
Though professional in tone.
I'm aching to my very core,
And feel so totally alone.

I see you lying comfortably,
Settled in your favourite place.
I make sure you have your treasured toy,
And are given dignity and grace?

Cowardly, I ask you for a sign,
Please make your instruction clear.
Life without you by my side,
Is an intolerable fear.

One thing I know for certain,
And my final show of love.
Is to unearth the strength and do what's right,
Before angels carry you above.

Are the voices which surround me,
Correct in what they say?
This is unbearable, I need to know,
Kneeling by your side, I pray.

With rolling tears, and in my heart,
I realise that now it is the time.
I kiss you and hug you close,
Anxiety begins to climb.

Your expression says you're thanking me,
For giving you this gift.
For releasing all the tiredness,
And allowing your soul to lift.

A struggling glance across the room,
Sees me tearfully nod my head.
I'd give everything I own and more,
To erase the moment that I dread.

You lift your head and look around,
A paw alights my knee.
You give the biggest headbutt,
You're wanting to be free.

I kiss you for the final time,
The years replay before my eyes.
Surely yesterday you were a baby?
Yet now we're saying our goodbyes.

Your paw remains on my knee,
As you drift into eternal sleep.
Farewell my friend, my special one,
In my heart the memories I'll keep.

Despite my utter heartbreak,
The despair, the grief and tears.
You enriched my life and taught me well,
Throughout those glorious years.

A quietness settles around me,
I look through the window above.
Sunbeams shine so brightly,
Your final gift of love.

You're showing me that you're content,
A spirit now at peace.
The angels have you in their arms,
You needed this release.

I want the outside world to know,
That on the day when pets depart.
The people they have left behind,
Lose a huge piece of their heart.

Take your time to listen ,
And expect their heart to break in two.
Be the best friend that you can be now,
That's all they ask of you.

© Hazel Prosser 2022

EMOTIONAL CONFETTI

When my emotions are raw, I almost always turn to writing - which is exactly what happened on the day I lost George.

I was bereft and had never been engulfed in such a tidal wave of emtoion, so I began to type my feelings, hoping that by doing so, I would feel at the very least, a little understanding and perhaps some solace.

The words of 'Emotional Confetti' convey how I was feeling at that moment, with the passing of George still so keenly felt.

When one shares their life with pets, it is observed that no matter how many you love, there will be always be one who grabs a little extra piece of your heart. For me, that was George.

Initially, I used the word 'splintered' instead of 'confetti', but that sounded so sharp and harsh, when George was soft and gentle. Confetti, gently fluttering down felt more appropriate, particularly as my emotions were scattered in the same way confetti is at a wedding or celebration.

Having loved and lost many animals, it's not something you ever become accustomed to so with 'Emotional Confetti' I was remembering not only how special George was, but also reassuring myself that eventually the pain would dull, and I would be able to reflect with fondness on the fun and fabulous times we shared.

EMOTIONAL CONFETTI

My heart's emotional confetti
As today the angels came.
And cradled my beloved cat,
For Heaven's eternal gain

Society doesn't understand,
They say "it's just a pet".
But I've lost a family member,
That's what they just don't get.

God above please tell me,
What am I to do?
I am praying for such strength,
That will guide and see me through.

Rest in peace my little one
My thanks for all you gave.
The joy, the laughter, the everything
In your honour I must be brave

There is a Rainbow Bridge
Where you'll walk across and wait
Until it's my time to join you
Through Heaven's pearly gate

Yes, my heart is broken!
But I need to say one thing.
I was blessed to love my special friend.
And enjoy the laughter he did bring.

Time will ease my burden,
And dilute my pain and sorrow,
I'll embrace the glorious memories,
Which will gild each new tomorrow.

© *Hazel Prosser 2009*

HOUSEWORK DAY

During the worst of times, life goes on regardless and housework is one mundanity that will always be there. On a beautiful summer morning I found myself in the throes of housework, cleaning every conceivable inch of my house in an effort to distract myself from grief. Hugo - my longstanding housework buddy - would no longer be joining me.

Hugo, unlike most cats, was never fazed by the noise and bustle of the hoover. Whilst Henry and Heidi slept upstairs, Hugo would be wherever I was, weaving his chubby paws around my ankles and becoming one gorgeous furry trip hazard.

In some ways, housework was playtime for Hugo. The light on the front of the vacuum cleaner would be fair game as he chased it around the room - much like one of those laser pointer toys.

This particular day was my first doing the housework alone which meant it was taking longer than usual. Caught up in memories and emotions, my feet dragged, missing the sometimes imovable object they'd often stumbled over. When I eventually reached the lounge I moved the armchair to make sure I collected any lurking crumbs from beneath, and it was then that I found it - a toy mouse. A small catnip toy mouse. Hugo's small catnip toy mouse.

I caught my breath as a familiar pain stabbed at my heart, then suddenly, it eased, disappearing beneath an overwhelming warmth which flowed through my entire being. I thought of Hugo leaving his mouse there just for me to find, almost as a reminder that he was always going to be with me.

Especially on housework day.

HOUSEWORK DAY

It's here again is housework day,
Various chores to do!
I'm picking up, packing up, washing up,
And dusting 'til I'm through!

I reach down for the vacuum,
But freeze right on the spot …
You're not around my feet today,
And tying them in a knot!

Suddenly, I'm all alone,
I want you by my side.
Or watching me search for various toys,
You took great delight to hide!

You really did love housework day,
To you it was such fun!
You felt it was your given right,
To undo the work, I'd done!

You'd race into the garden,
Returning with little muddy paws!
I'd find your bespoke signature,
All over my sparkling clean floors!

You'd jump upon the countertop,
Ignoring my clear protestation!
Looking at me quizzically,
Demanding an explanation!

Clean laundry was your favourite,
Especially the folded sheets and towels.
Neatness was unnecessary,
According to your playful little growls!

Thank you for the memories,
Intricately carved throughout the years.
So yes, I know I'm smiling,
Through the rolling stream of tears.

I continue doing all the chores,
But, as I move the chair.
Curiously, I spy one little toy,
I believe you meant it to be there!

Charming memories such as these,
Locked tight inside my heart.
Proves even on the mundane days,
Never shall we part.

© Hazel Prosser 2022

WINTER WANDERING ... & WONDERING

In my garden, I have created memorials for beloved animals who are no longer with me. These memorials are carefully designed to blend in with their surroundings, yet each one has a special meaning. After losing George, for instance, I decided to plant a purple hazel tree as he had lilac-colourpoints on his fur and my name is, well, Hazel. Next to this tree there is a beautiful rose bush which blooms with vibrant red flowers - the colour of love. When Hugo passed away, I planted a rose bush in his honour. The soft yellow petals of these flowers are a reflection of his gorgeous cream colour-pointed coat.

During the Winter of 2021, I wrote a poem called 'Winter Wandering' which was inspired by my garden. As I spent time outside, I was struck by the vivid blue sky which was reminiscent of the eye colour of both my boys. The cold snap of weather seemed to heighten my emotions and before long I was engulfed in sadness, thinking of my gorgeous cats.

Glancing at the hazel tree, though, and then onto the rose bushes helped immensely, the shrubs I had planted so lovingly bringing me a sense of peace and comfort.

I genuinely believe that animals are the greatest of teachers; those I have loved (and lost) and continue to love, have taught me so much.

The stillness of my garden along with the wonder of George and Hugo's memorials, have brought me solace during the most difficult of times.

WINTER WANDERING ... & WONDERING

The winter sun shines brightly,
Crouching low in frosty sky.
I wander around our garden,
Birds chorus, in trees up high.

I glance over at the rose bush,
Under which you rest eternally.
How I wish with all my heart,
That you were still here with me.

I whisper to you so softly,
Into the crisp and icy air.
I love you more than you'll ever know,
And silently, I say a prayer.

As I look up to the sky above,
Shimmering blue just like your eyes,
I feel your presence near me,
But the grief I cannot disguise.

I remember all you taught me,
More than any school to which I went,
The lesson was to embrace each day,
And not to waste a moment lent.

I realise now what I must do,
To honour your love and memory,
I am to take each day, as it presents itself,
Rather than worry about "what may never be".

© Hazel Prosser 2020

SECTION TWO

Poetry for

HOLIDAYS, ANNIVERSARIES & DIFFICULT TIMES

(including anticipatory grief)

ANNIVERSARIES

I think most of us can remember the exact date when our beloved person or pet passed away. And because of that, we feel a sense of sadness and grief whenever that date comes around, no matter how much time has passed.

The first anniversary is definitely emotional. It marks a whole year without that special person or beloved animal who meant so much to us. This initial year and anniversary will almost certainly be particularly challenging and from thereon, every anniversary will serve as a reminder, prompting us to take a moment and reflect.

For me, on those particular anniversaries, I try and do something that the one I miss would enjoy: travel to a place of special meaning to them, or if it's an animal, sit in the garden and remember.

If you are facing an anniversary or, if today is an anniversary, then why not consider doing something meaningful to honour their memory? It may be as simple as putting a favourite photograph in a lovely new frame, planting a rose bush or taking a walk somewhere that you both enjoyed.

Just something special for you and them on this day.

ANNIVERSARIES

There's a sinking feeling inside,
And a single wandering tear.
The dawn of today, heralds,
Your anniversary year.

Time has passed,
Life forced to move on,
Memories in the world,
I've created since you've been gone.

Today I'll spend it reminiscing,
Looking up to the widest of skies.
Wishing with every breath in my body,
I could see your gentle blue eyes.

Now you are cradled with angels
Who spoke on this anniversary day,
Whispering in your ear that,
You were far too precious to stay.

They watched you make my life,
Such a serene and beautiful place.
With your ever-calm demeanour
Your presence and your grace.

"Your work has been done,"
They smiled, speaking with such love.
"From here on in my precious,
You'll look down from high above."

Until the time of reckoning
When we'll meet once again,
I take comfort in all those signs,
You send, to soak up my pain.

You live on in my heart,
And that's just where you will stay.
For all of eternity,
Not only on this anniversary day.

© Hazel Prosser 2022

THE ETERNAL CHRISTMAS CARD

Christmas can be an incredibly challenging time for those who are grieving. The words 'happy' and 'merry' are particularly difficult to hear, representing as they do, emotions which may feel out of reach at that time.

Personally, I have experienced many Christmases grieving, trying my best to stay emotionally afloat amidst the festivities. The arrival of cheerful cards with their festive messages provide a sage reminder of a loved one's absence, and their well-intentioned sentiments often bring forth painful emotions that are intensified by the relentless backdrop of jollity.

I have found, over the years, that it is more comforting to email or call someone who I know is going to be finding Christmas difficult. I do this rather than sending cards because I feel it is a more appropriate reminder of them being in my thoughts, than a poorly-timed colourful card which oozes brightly coloured happiness. It's helpful to remember, I feel, that not everyone is feeling festive simply because it is Christmas Day.

Reflections on this led me to write 'The Eternal Christmas Card'. My intention was to allow those we miss to be included within our celebrations and to bring comfort to those left behind.

Please use this poem as needed, especially if you know someone who will be struggling during the festive season.

> *"Close the card and with all my love,*
> *Have yourself a wonderful Christmas Day."*

THE ETERNAL CHRISTMAS CARD

I've received a special Christmas card,
From my loved one up above.
Tenderly written sentiments,
Delivered with so much love.

The words I read in silence,
They're beautiful and sincere.
Acknowledging an absence,
Intensified at this time of year.

"Please know that I am with you,
Cast aside your regrets and fears.
I sent an angel to warm your soul,
And wipe away the tears.

Christmas is togetherness,
Twinkling lights on every tree.
Embrace each moment that you can,
Would you do that just for me?

We enjoyed such special moments,
And whilst the holidays feel so hard.
For this year and future Christmases,
Just read the words inside this card.

In my new world there's so much joy,
A warmth of festive cheer.
Yet, our bond will never come undone,
It's embroidered into every year.

Now you've read the words I've gifted,
And listened to all I say.
Close the card, and with all my love,
Have yourself a wonderful Christmas Day!"

© Hazel Prosser 2023

THE PRICELESS GIFT

I wrote 'The Priceless Gift' just before the first Christmas after Hugo's passing. I recall returning from shopping and feeling low because I couldn't get used to his absence. Writing this poem helped me to process my feelings and understand that Hugo (and all of my feline companions) wouldn't want me to be sad. Especially not at Christmas.

'The Priceless Gift' conveys the message that our pets are still by our side, watching over us. They may miss us, but they don't want us to grieve. They love us and want to comfort us, and let us know that they are okay, even though they are no longer visible to us in our world.

No matter what, our pets will always leave behind their legacy and more than that, the most valuable Christmas gift of all …

Love ♥

THE PRICELESS GIFT

I watched you return from your shopping spree,
Bags scattered across the floor.
I saw you sigh, your shoulders heavy,
Fervently, I do implore.

"Please don't let this time of year,
Stop you from including me.
I haven't left your side, or home,
I'm here, where I'll always be."

You move your purchases from place to place,
Tears bubbling in your eyes.
"I miss you, my little one", you cry,
Which takes me by surprise!

You seat yourself in our favourite chair,
I curl up between your feet.
You look at all the shopping,
And willingly admit defeat.

My view beyond your shoulder,
Extends to the world outside,
I see festive trees and coloured lights,
Yet within these walls you hide.

Conspicuous by my absence,
That came as such a blow.
Be reassured, I am happy still
It was just my time to go.

Please go and unpack your items,
Conceal them in paper with pretty bows.
I'll watch you with fascination,
To see where each one goes!

When you are done, fill up the kettle,
Make a comforting cup of tea.
But before you do, I have one request.
"Wrap a gift for me."

Our mutual gift is priceless,
No need for currency.
Nor all that fancy wrapping,
Because we share our love. Eternally.

© *Hazel Prosser 2021*

WE ARE ONE - NEW YEAR MESSAGE

I wrote this poem on New Year's Eve 2021, but, from the perspective of those who have left this world and are looking down on their loved ones. As a reminder of the many New Year's Eve's where together they waited in eager anticipation to welcome in the approaching year.

When I wrote this I needed reassurance. It was the year I reached my fiftieth birthday, and where the world was still at the mercy of the pandemic. I found myself in deep reflection and decided to uncover old photo albums which hadn't seen the light of day for years. I wanted to bathe in happy memories by looking at images from another time and watching old cinefilm movies. I wanted to experience the wonder of those times once more, though the pain was constant when familiar faces now missing, were a reminder of how precious life is.

Those who are no longer with us may wish they could offer reassurance as we continue our journey without them and this poem, does that - by communicating their perceived message in a way that feels appropriate.

Writing this gave me much comfort. In an ever-changing world, 'We Are One' is a reminder that no matter what the day, we never leave those we love behind.

WE ARE ONE - NEW YEAR MESSAGE

Our home is still,
The clock ticks away,
Your heart is heavy,
Since I left that day.

I feel the sadness,
In the magnitude of every tear.
As in your head,
You rewind each year.

To the joyous life
The fun we shared,
The together times
Unimpaired.

I yearn to lift that burden,
You carry like chains.
And convince you that forever,
Our love sustains.

When you reflect on the life
We enjoyed so dear,
Look at our photos,
And what you'll see is clear.

*You'll start to smile,
And I'll beam with pride,
Then watch for signs,
Proving I'm at your side.*

*The new year arrives,
It's simply another tomorrow,
And just like today
It's only time we borrow.*

*So when you're feeling low,
And emotions are blue.
Place your hand on your heart,
Because, I'm right there with you.*

© Hazel Prosser 2021

WILL YOU SAVE ME A PLACE THIS CHRISTMAS?

How do *you* feel about the holiday season? Do you enjoy it or not?

It's common for us to embrace Christmas with an array of festivities and spend time with family, but what if there is a family member missing this year? What if it's the first Christmas without them? Or a time of year when the loss of a loved one feels especially painful?

Christmas seems to come earlier each year. Shops stock their shelves with all kinds of goodies, however for those who are grieving, this time of year can bring heightened emotions - something which others may simply not understand.

Off-the-cuff comments such as, "Bah! Humbug!" can be extremely unhelpful and only adds to the weight of loss and guilt that those who are struggling already feel.

The comforting thought of still having our loved ones near is what inspired me to write this poem presented as a chat, a conversation between those living and those no longer here. I wanted to let them know that they will always have a place reserved at the Christmas dinner table - as well as in my home and my heart.

These words, I hope, will provide solace for you too, as you navigate a time of year that can be fraught with difficulty.

WILL YOU SAVE ME A PLACE THIS CHRISTMAS?

"Will you save me a place this Christmas …
Now I'm in a new celestial realm?"
"Will you save me a place this Christmas …
When emotions overwhelm?"

I'll save you a place this Christmas,
In every cheery festive song.
I'll save you a place this Christmas,
For together we belong.

I'll save you a place this Christmas,
In the glowing lights so bright.
I'll save you a place this Christmas,
When day turns into night.

I'll save you a place this Christmas,
An exquisite present by the tree.
I'll save you a place this Christmas,
Wishing you were here with me.

I'll save you a place this Christmas,
Even though we're two worlds apart.
I'll save you a place this Christmas,
In my home, my soul, my heart ♥.

ON THE CUSP OF TOMORROW
~ ANTICIPATORY GRIEF ~

Have you ever experienced 'Anticipatory Grief'? I have, regrettably on several occasions, which is why my heart breaks for anyone currently in this situation. Like death, this is another subject I feel we don't address or talk about with the level of openness we should. I hope, therefore, that the words contained within the lines of this poem, reach out and touch you.

'On the Cusp of Tomorrow' was initially written for pet loss, but I wanted it to be more generic, so, in the first and second verses there is the acknowledgment of grief for the 'one I love', which could relate equally to both pets and humans.

Interestingly, I wrote this poem in stages, almost verse by verse, because I wanted to use it as a way of explaining feelings during this difficult time. When we are awaiting the inevitable departure of a loved one, it can be hard for others to really understand, so I wanted to try and sum up, line by line, the different stages of anticipatory grief based on my experience.

I think the main learning I have gained from each of my heartbreaking losses, is the importance of living every single day and making the most of each moment. Even if we know that a loss is coming soon - perhaps even more so at this time - I firmly believe we should make those final days the very best that we can. And, one small way we can do that, is to help those closest to us to understand how we are feeling.

I really hope that 'On the Cusp of Tomorrow' achieves this.

ON THE CUSP OF TOMORROW
~ ANTICIPATORY GRIEF ~

I watch you through misty eyes,
Trying to stay strong.
My heart yearns to keep you here,
Yet I know you've not got long.

I'm grieving for the one I love,
Whilst you're still here by my side
I feel so isolated,
In a way I can't abide.

We've spent so many happy years,
Enjoying our life of fun.
Now the years could be months, or days,
Life's predicted setting sun.

Intent on making every single day,
As special as can be,
"Where there's life, there's certain hope."
I whisper emotionally.

Friends tell me how they "understand".
But I don't believe that's true.
How can they really comprehend?
The love I have for you.

Today has dawned with shimmering light.
Sun, above the parapet
Beaming rays bathe your velvet coat.
Angels kissing you, I fret.

It's said the eyes reflect the soul.
So, you'll know there'll never be.
A unity as strong as ours
Not another "You and Me"

In my grief there's gratitude
For we've always been a team
We'll cherish every moment gifted.
Letting nothing intervene

I want to grab the hands of time.
And stop them going round.
To get off this rollercoaster ride
And keep you safe and sound.

Talking sternly to my emotions
I tell them to wait until it's time.
Admiring your fighting spirit
I'm so proud that you are mine.

© Hazel Prosser 2022

SECTION THREE

Poetry for
FAMILY

TIME MOVES ON – THE FIRST MONTH

The first month after Mum's passing seemed to evaporate. As with previous bereavements, I couldn't see where one day began and another ended. Predictably I had many 'W' questions running through my mind.

"**WHAT**" questions:

"What more could I have done for you?"
"What did I miss?"
"What am I going to do without you?"
"What is to become of me?"
"What did I not say to you?"

"**WHY**" questions:

"Why has this happened? (to you/me)"
"Why am I feeling so lost/angry/alone/defensive/isolated/powerless/helpless?"
"Why didn't I ask more questions?"
"Why didn't I notice signs earlier?"
"Why is life so unfair?"

"**WHEN**" questions:

"When am I going to stop grieving?"
"When will the tears subside?"
"When will I stop feeling so angry?"
"When will this pain lessen?"
"When am I ever going to be myself again?"

"**WHO**" questions:

"Who am I without you?"
"Whose fault is this?"
"Who will ever understand how I'm feeling?"
"Who will prove, through all adversity to be a real friend?"
"Who will help me when I need it?"

"**WHERE**" questions:

"Where did I go wrong?"
"Where are you?"
"Where do I turn now?"
"Where is there useful support?"
"Where am I going?"

As well as questioning myself, I began to question my faith when I saw how much Mum struggled. In fact, I questioned everything in that first month as grief turned into anger and then bitterness at how unfair life was.

Though the reference to my landline telephone may seem odd, it is poignant because I only kept it for Mum's use. She much preferred calling me on that because I'd had the same number since the mid-1990's and she knew it off by heart.

Mum would also say that animals were the truest of friends, and in my animals I see that every day. Patiently and quietly standing by, offering comfort without judgement.

At Mum's funeral a dear friend told me to keep a candle burning in my heart for Mum, so that she will never be forgotten.

I have. And this candle is inextinguishable.

TIME MOVES ON - THE FIRST MONTH

A month has passed already.
My world exists in disbelief.
The life I knew upended.
Suffocated by endless tears of grief.

How can time just run away?
Like the finest grains of sand,
It feels like only yesterday,
I gently held your fragile hand.

You fought so hard to the end.
With a spirit brave and strong.
On an endless loop, I question,
Just what did I do wrong?

What more could I have done for you?
What words did I not say?
My prayers went unanswered.
Why could God not let you stay?

To describe your life, "a rollercoaster,"
So much of it unfair,
I only wish I'd said more often,
How deeply that I cared.

What I would give for one more day
Or even an hour or two
To say all the things I should have done.
Whilst I was there with you

I exist in deafening silence.
My landline no longer rings,
I yearn for those lengthy conversations.
When we talked through so many things

I am a kaleidoscope of turmoil.
As I sit with a cat or two upon my knee,
Inside my head, I hear your words,
"Give them both a hug from me."

Your footsteps, I will walk in
The passage of time will see me through,
A candle alight within my heart
Is kept there just for you.

© Hazel Prosser 2022

A LIFE FOREVER CHANGED

I have never been a fan of New Year's Eve. There, I've said it.

The revelry after the stress and hype of Christmas, is too much for me - especially as the 31st of December is one of my biggest trigger dates. As each year draws to a close I am flooded with memories.

'A Life Forever Changed' was written on the 31st of December 2022. I sat alone with my thoughts, only this year felt worse than ever as I was reflecting on the pain of losing mum. My heart was breaking, yet, as I have said often, writing has become such a powerful mode of expression for me so it was only natural that night, for me to embroider Mum's strong faith into these words.

She was my first home, my safety, my comfort, my strength and it was through her that I became the person I am today. 'A Life Forever Changed' is a tribute, an acknowledgement of everything we shared and a thankfulness to have known her.

Without our parents, we would be nothing, and though my life has forever been changed, I take pride and comfort in this book, these poems, this gift - because it is my way of making sure those I've lost are never forgotten.

I hope you can find yourself within these verses, discover those you have loved and lost and then remember them. Hear their words once more as you celebrate their legacy.

When Big Ben strikes each year, I know I am not leaving anyone behind and nor are you. Our loved ones are with us always.

A LIFE FOREVER CHANGED

A poignant date on the calendar
Brings to a close ,the most distressing of years
My heart so leaden and heavy
Eyes collecting a river of tears

This year dementia threw a shroud over my life
Consuming my Mother with all of its might
Her life one of hard working honesty
Became like a dimmable light

Dementia is inexplicable to outsiders
Just a word in a medical book
Having to witness dramatic change in one's Mother
Her pained, confused, frustrated outlook

Twelve months ago, she was driving
Or enjoying walks with a little dog at her side
Each day as dementia gripped tighter
The life she once knew it would bitterly hide

Despite the cruel fate which befell Mum
She never once complained or questioned the change
When I visited on many occasions
I saw her slipping further from discernible range

Thankfully, Mum never totally forgot me
But for a year I saw a life fading away
The sands of time in her life ran so furiously
Every morning and night I would pray

I would pray for the fogginess to disperse
And for my Mum to return with such force
But because of the nemesis this condition is
All that could happen, was for it to run out its course

Mum always told me that "life was for living"
And never "just to exist"
But what dementia does with its venom
Is to make one live when the real you is missed

In September God called Mum to rest
In deep sleep she entered his care
Every animal and person who ever loved her
I know was waiting to welcome her there

This year is at an imminent close
The chimes from Big Ben will soon signal its end
And I know Mum will be waiting to greet me
When the time comes for me to transcend

We can never truly be parted
She has moved to a new address I can't as yet see
But my heart it beats for us both
Because without my Mother, there would not be me.

LISTEN TO YOUR HEART

This poem, and I hope I don't sound self-indulgent, is one of which I am incredibly proud. Written at such a heart-breaking time in my life: the loss of my mother.

When one loses a Parent, it gives a sense of personal mortality, together with the realisation of how precious life is and how fragile each day truly is.

From the moment the date was arranged for Mum's funeral, I knew I wanted to read a eulogy. Whilst I had words in my head, I was unsure if I would be able to summon the strength to speak them, but I was determined not to let her down.

On that day, I read this poem and though I faltered, I know I did her life justice. Afterwards, I was complimented by many who said I had created the perfect words, not just for me as a grieving daughter, but for all in their time of grief. Since then, I have been asked on many occasions to create bespoke poetry for others and 'Listen to Your Heart,' has become a comfort. It is generic enough for all and precious enough to me, written, as it was, as a gift to my parents, animals and everyone else I have loved and lost.

I hope this poem speaks to you and that just as I will, you will remember to be strong when obstacles come your way …

> … *"And if ever you question what to do,*
> *just listen to your heart".*

LISTEN TO YOUR HEART

*Sit in silence,
And remember me.
But not with tears or pain.
Recall those many happy times,
With a purity that will sustain.*

*We may not be together,
In the physical sense, I know,
Life it turns full circle,
And in time, each of us must go.*

*We will always be in unity,
For our ties can never fray.
An embroidered thread binds our souls,
It was destined to be this way.*

*Take each new day, embrace it,
I taught you from the start.
And if ever you question what to do,
Just listen to your heart.*

© Hazel Prosser 2022

LUCKY SIXPENCE

I grew up listening to 'old wives tales' and fables. I would look for four-leaf clovers, salute magpies and avoid walking under ladders - to name a few. These stories often creep into my poems, I've realised, and 'Lucky Sixpence' is one example, where I am creatively re-telling a real-life experience.

During a childhood trip to Birmingham with my father, I came across a old coin lying on the ground. My dad, wearing a mischievous grin, humorously suggested that I pick it up for 'good luck'.

"See a penny, pick it up, all day long, you'll have good luck". He said. So I picked it up.

My father proceeded to explain the significance of the lucky sixpence and the tradition of placing these coins in Christmas puddings. I found it captivating how such a small coin was believed to bring luck and blessings for the forthcoming year.

The concept of coins being regarded as fortunate, even those discarded, appealed to me and Dad's words have remained etched in my memory.

Coins may bring luck and we certainly work hard enough to earn them, but friends, family and even animals hold a special charm in our lives which have a value that is truly priceless.

LUCKY SIXPENCE

*I found a little sixpence,
Just lying on the ground.
A coin from days of yesteryear,
Waiting to be found.*

*A rhyme of old suggests it's lucky,
To pick up a penny, you may find.
But to see an unusual sixpence,
Brought a thought into my mind.*

*My eyes looked to the heavens,
A tear crystallised and fell.
You're showing me a precious sign,
And telling me all is well.*

*I reach for the little sixpence,
The sun radiates from the sky.
This little coin glints so bright,
I exhale the deepest sigh.*

*Childhood memories flood my head,
With stories from days gone by.
About the shining sixpence,
Its luck, and the reasons why.*

This coin becomes my lucky charm,
Because that's what you were to me.
A love which not only lasts a lifetime,
But throughout all eternity.

THE EMOTIONAL CAROUSEL

This poem combines my childhood memories with an open-air museum called Blists Hill which is a place I love. It is located in a Victorian town in Shropshire, England and I go there as often as I can to enjoy the spectacle of a bygone era. Here, I can be alone with my thoughts and memories and I find it incredibly healing to "step out of the 21st century" for a while.

On one occasion, I was standing by the Carousel (or 'Merry-go-Round' as it is often called) when memories of childhood were awakened. I remembered the times when I would rush forwards and clamber eagerly onto a horse, my father lifting me up when I was too small to get up on my own. "You must hold tight," he would say.

These memories caused me to smile as I watched the carousel spin, then suddenly, I experienced an overwhelming sense of guilt. Guilt that I had allowed myself a moment of happiness, and that I was still alive and able to enjoy life when others who I have loved, were not.

Guilt is an element of grief I have struggled with, so when I wrote this poem I wanted to convey those feelings - which led me to realise that in fact, it was okay for me to have times of happiness, and that my loved ones did not want me to always be sad. Smiling and having fun didn't mean I was forgetting those I had lost, quite the opposite in fact. It meant I was honouring them by continuing to live through mine and their shared memories.

THE EMOTIONAL CAROUSEL

A rare trip to the funfair,
Sensory explosions all around,
The carousel in its splendour,
Yet, I don't hear a sound.

I watch the horses rise and fall,
My emotions do the same.
Reliving fondest childhood days
When life was just a game!

To some extent, I'm in a trance,
De-sensitised from fun.
Feeling oh so guilty
Without you, my precious one.

Life is a personal 'merry-go-round',
Each moment powered by grief.
One moment I am feeling fine,
The next, numb with disbelief.

What right have I to be watching,
Hand-crafted majesty?
Smiling, being entertained,
Without you at home to welcome me.

Up and down, and round and round
The horses go all day.
It's pretty much how I would describe
My life, since you went away.

Glancing at the vintage amusement park,
With its myriad of rides,
Side stalls and coconut shies.
Twisting helter-skelter slides.

The carousel comes to a halt
Allowing riders to disembark,
Smiles light up their faces,
"What fun!" is the collective remark.

Now stationary the horses look forlorn,
As I walk up to their sides.
Silently I feel the urge,
To take one for a ride!

I climb upon my chosen steed,
In a livery of white, gold and red.
As if by magic a butterfly appears,
Settling on the horse's wooden head.

The carousel cranks up once again,
I am transported to bygone days,
The air perfumed by sugary treats,
My eyes blinking a teary glaze.

Despite the ride's momentum,
The butterfly stays calm,
Elegant wings are on parade,
A serene, spiritually gifted charm.

Spellbound, I don't realise,
When the ride has come to an end.
The butterfly rises and lands upon my arm,
And I know it's you, my devoted -friend.

Spiritual threads that bind us tight,
Bring the winged messenger from above.
To gently tell me all is well,
And surround me with your love.

© Hazel Prosser 2022

THE FIRST ANNIVERSARY
(Words of a Grieving Daughter)

This is one of the most personal poems I have included, and it was a tough call as to whether I should do so or not. But, my Mother gave me life and made me who I am so I wanted to honour her by offering these few lines to other Daughters (or Sons) who may be mourning their own losses, too.

Every anniversary, including seasonal holidays and birthdays, are tough. There's a huge hole where your loved one once was and the 'firsts' are, in my experience, always the hardest.

On the 30th of September 2023, the first anniversary of my mother's passing, I offloaded my grief by writing, and this poem is the end result. I wanted to remind Mum just how much she meant to me and I wanted to let her know that she still guides me. Every single day.

For those of you in a similar situation, I would like to think there are words within this poem that resonate, and that you can attribute it to your loved ones too.

THE FIRST ANNIVERSARY
(Words of a Grieving Daughter)

I've awoken with a heavy heart,
Remembering how a year ago today
I held your hand and kissed your cheek,
Emotions in turmoil as you slipped away.

God looked down and saw the struggle.
You'd endured for far too long.
He whispered to the angels.
"This lady no longer needs to be strong".

The angels nodded in agreement,
They knew the time was right.
Gently, you were carried onwards,
Bathed in celestial golden light.

The angels gain was incomprehensible,
I'm now a daughter without her Mum.
And without you here to guide me,
Whatever will I become?

I cannot believe a year has passed,
The first of many more.
What I would give for *one* last chance,
To see you standing at my door.

I envy those who will embrace,
Enjoyable and fun-filled years.
Whilst I sit alone with a broken heart,
My eyes pools of burning tears.

I miss you Mum, I always will,
But know this much is true.
The person that I am today,
I am because of you.

I talk about you with so much pride,
*There will **never** be another.*
No-one can fill the void,
Of you, my uniquely special Mother.

© Hazel Prosser 2023

Original Artwork ©Bill Prosser

LIVE EVERY DAY AS IF IT WERE YOUR LAST

In the same way as 'Lucky Sixpence', this poem was inspired by memories of my dad. He possessed sharp wit, intelligence, artistic talent and a wealth of knowledge, however he could be emotionally withdrawn, too. As a pre-World War II baby, Dad belonged to a generation who did not show emotions. Many of his friends lost their fathers during the first World War, however dad lost his due to its after-effects. "Dad was gassed in the war," he would say. As a child I had no idea what this meant, other than the fact that my grandfather had died.

In later years, watching the film 'War Horse', I finally understood exactly what 'being gassed' meant, and I experienced so much sadness at what my grandfather must have gone through and what my dad had lost.

At the age of fourteen, dad left school which was the norm back then. The year was 1939. As he had no father, the expectation was for him to support his widowed mother (along with his siblings), so they each took as many odd jobs as they could to help make ends meet. Back then, there was no financial assistance available like there is today. What I always found remarkable once I fully appreciated his story, was that he never showed any bitterness at what his life had been. He simply kept looking forwards.

During National Service, (a requirement for all men of legal age), dad served in the Royal Engineers. I remember his hands being scarred - outward reminders of what he had seen - yet it is undoubtedly true that even greater damage was done on the inside. Counselling and support for soldiers was not available back then; they simply did their duty and, if they were lucky enough to return home, tried their best to leave everything behind and continue with a 'normal' life. This is how it was and

I am sure contributed to the 'stiff upper lip' for which us Brits are well known.

I realise now that there was so much grief my father experienced, most of which could never be anticipated. With no option to unburden himself, I sensed his unhappiness at times, though he would always put on a bright smile. He used his dry and quick humour to turn any situation around and inject light where there may have been dark. Even today I don't know how he managed to cope with the demons that must have plagued him. To the uninitiated observer he kept them under lock and key, always deflecting unwanted conversations and maintaining a stoic silence about how he truly felt.

Dad spent fifty years as an electrician at an aluminium factory located in Kitts Green, which is a suburb of Birmingham, and the thought of leaving never crossed his mind - another sign of the times. It was the most natural thing in the world for him to dedicate his life to the factory and though he never learned to drive, it didn't stop him from taking me all over the place on the bus. It is through him I gained my love of history and I've often pondered if his passion for history and antiques stemmed from a longing to relive his childhood and happy days before National Service.

Whenever dad referred to the 'good old days', I instinctively knew that these were the ones he was talking about and that they were cherished and held, deep within his heart.

LIVE EVERY DAY AS IF IT WERE YOUR LAST

I wonder, did you ever know,
When, as a child, I sat upon your knee.
Teaching me how to read and write,
And recite my ABC.

That every word you endearingly spoke,
And precious memories you once shared,
Would shape the person I would become?
But never was I prepared ...

To say goodbye to the man whose life,
Had been forged out of toil and chore.
A child who saw his own Father,
Succumb to the consequences of The Great War.

A young man, you were called for National Service,
Commanded to "Relinquish all your fears".
Your duties stationed in a foreign land,
A brave Sapper of the Royal Engineers.

You never spoke much about those days,
Or the horrors there must have been.
I knew not to ask too many questions,
In case emotions had cause to intervene.

Then, for fifty years, a factory worker
A skilled Electrician to earn your money.
In the city of Birmingham, you loved so much
Never was there a prouder Brummie!

You always had a thirst for knowledge,
A passion for antiques and history."
We live in a Country rich with heritage,"
You used to say to me.

When you weren't enjoying our history,
Or visiting museums and galleries of art.
You'd sit and create your own paintings,
With hands so talented and a brain so smart.

The day came all too soon, it's true,
One I refused to believe I'd ever see.
Perched on the edge of your hospital bed, I whispered,
"One day, Dad, I'll make you proud of me".

More than two decades of time now, since that day,
It's unbelievable how years go so fast.
But the best advice you ever shared,
"Live every day as if it were your last."

© Hazel Prosser 2024

MY FINAL WISH

I wrote this poem because I wanted to address an often sensitive subject - namely our own mortality. For me, it's not maudlin. I've always been comfortable talking about death, right from the first time I asked my dad what it was all about.

"At what age do we die, daddy?" I asked. He chose to answer honestly, for which I have always been grateful.

"At any age," he replied.

"Even babies?"

"Unfortunately, yes".

As children do, I continued to ask question after question, until eventually he gave me this answer:

"Nipper," he said, "we are dying from the day we are born. Live every day as if it were your last, because one day it will be."

From that moment on, I understood that life ends in death and I accepted this as a non-negotiable, something we cannot swerve.

I wish that we spoke more openly about death, the way I did that day with my dad. Often, though we understand its inevitability, we are unprepared, which can lead to many difficult and unanswered questions.

'My Final Wish' is a weaving of my own desires into a poem which also, I believe, opens up the dialogue for you, my reader. I hope it resonates and in some ways gives you permission to have those difficult conversations now, whilst we still can.

MY FINAL WISH

When my earthly time is at an end,
Reassure yourselves knowing this …
I shall be going to those who wait for me,
Faithfully, loyally and who I do so miss.

There'll be Mum & Dad's welcome as I transcend,
Those 'pearly gates' they'll walk me through.
But to take in my arms, each four legged friend,
Will be my final wish, come true.

No headstone will identify my resting place,
No plaque in my Royal town of birth.
My ashes will feed a tree which bears my name,
Returning me to God's blessed earth.

Be encouraged when you read my words,
My life has always been forward thought.
"Live every day as if it were your last,"
For life really is very short.

My heart has many paw prints,
Adorning its every space.
Since the moment I arrived into this world,
I've always known a pet's embrace.

For now, life is for living,
To walk a path already trod.
By those who have gone before me,
And are now in the hands of God.

I'll create many brand new memories,
As I journey through.
Broadening my horizons,
Is what I'm destined to.

For all of you who have read my book,
Much gratitude from me.
I hope there's a poem to comfort you,
Written with care and sincerity.

© Hazel Prosser 2023

SECTION FOUR

Poetry for
(ALL) TIMES OF GRIEF

BONDED

I wrote this poem from the perspective of an individual, be they human or pet, who is deeply cherished but no longer present, watching from the heavens to observe how the grieving person is managing, especially after a considerable duration has elapsed.

What they behold is their beloved human feeling disappointed by those they once trusted to provide support; as such, the departed loved one sends words of wisdom to their former companion from their new world.

They express pride in the shared history and emphasise that others may not comprehend the depth of their connection, as each individual is unique.

The message conveys a sense of eternal bond and reassures that their love will endure indefinitely and not to expect too much from others who may genuinely not understand.

BONDED

I saw you looking so forlorn,
Because time has now elapsed.
Those you thought that you could trust,
View me as a memory of the past.

Their once kind and sympathetic words,
Are now no more than bland.
For sadly they have no idea,
Or the desire to understand.

Though, it's true I've been gone a while,
Special dates have left their scar.
Don't listen to those who close their minds,
Or communicate from afar.

Feel thankful they don't comprehend,
The love we shared so deep.
The years of fun and joy were ours,
Before I discreetly fell asleep.

You and I share unbreakable ties,
And I talk in present tense.
Because our bond is forever and a day,
Yet to others this makes no sense.

So to those who will not take the time,
To understand a griever's love.
Just know the one they adored so much,
Beams with pride from up above.

There are billions of people on this earth,
Yet fate brought them together.
And the love that's shared in waking life,
Lives on in hearts forever.

© Hazel Prosser 2023

TALK TO ME ... LET MY NAME LIVE ON

"I wasn't sure if I should mention ..."

"I thought if I talked about ... it would upset you?"

It can be difficult for others to know what to say around those who have been bereaved. From my perspective, I believe the ones we have lost would wish to be talked about; they lived a life which was real, however short or long, and they were here with us on this earth.

I often talk to those I miss, not least because it helps me keep them 'alive' but also, it is my opinion that they do still hear us.

I appreciate, though, that talking to loved ones you have lost can be difficult - you may feel silly talking to what is effectively 'thin air', for example - which is why I wrote this poem. Reading it to yourself, or, if you feel comfortable, reading it aloud, will help you to maintain that precious communication with those you can no longer see.

Equally, if you are someone who talks to photographs, perhaps wishing them 'good morning' or 'goodnight', then you will find this poem a wonderful extension of this. It can help to cement the feelings you are already embracing.

Images in photos often mean everything to us, so I hope you can use these words alongside your own special images - even if they are only viewed in your mind - to remember those you have loved and lost, in a beautiful and peaceful way.

TALK TO ME ... LET MY NAME LIVE ON

I know your heart is breaking,
I see the tears flow.
Please don't feel guilty,
It was just my time to go.

My love for you is stronger,
With each new wondrous day.
I hear you talking to me,
Because I haven't gone away.

We're momentarily separated,
Through a veil which divides each realm.
I'm in your heart, and by your side,
When emotions overwhelm.

Talk to me, as you've always done,
When you've a moment going spare.
A love and bond as close as ours,
Is eternal and beyond compare.

So, when you keep my name alive,
I smile upon your heart.
That smile ignites our entwined souls,
Confirming that never shall we part.

© Hazel Prosser 2022

THE HEAVENLY CANDLE
(Illuminating My Heart)

Candles! I love them!

They possess a captivating and hypnotic quality which brings about a sense of tranquility and reverence. Living near the magnificent Lichfield Cathedral, I am fortunate to have the opportunity to light a candle whenever I visit. It serves as a way for me to honour and remember those who are no longer with me. I also offer a moment of prayer and reflection.

I find lighting a candle in my home infuses warmth into the room - no matter how big or small - and this warmth is how I perceive the love we share with our pets who bring comfort to our lives. Losing a pet will often cause a profound feeling of desolation, especially when returning to a quiet and empty home. When George passed away in 2009, my home felt vast and cold without him and it was only when Hugo joined my family that the warmth returned. My house was once again a home.

If you spend a moment watching the flame of a candle burning, you'll notice it resembles a teardrop shape, which is incredibly apt when we use it as such a poignant emblem of loss and cry hot tears of sorrow.

Originally written for the loss of a beloved pet, the sentiment of this poem can easily be extended to all who have left our lives.

THE HEAVENLY CANDLE
(Illuminating My Heart)

The gleaming candelabra,
Presides over the mantlepiece.
Ornate with glowing candles,
That never seem to cease.

Tiny, eager, flickering flames
A respectful show of love.
Radiate light from within my home,
To my best friend up above.

I soon begin to realise,
That each unique little flame
Is teardrop in shape and all a-glow,
My eyes erupt at Heaven's gain.

Whilst you were here, my house was a home,
And now that you have gone.
I'll light a candle in your honour,
And try to carry on.

There's one extra candle burning,
Invisibly concealed within my heart.
The warmth touches both our souls,
Uniting us though we are apart.

© Hazel Prosser 2023

UNIQUE AND PRECIOUS TIMES

This short poem was written as a snapshot of a lifetime of memories.

Life isn't always perfect, far from it, it can be difficult, frustrating and mundane as well as being fun and enjoyable with good times to share.

'Unique and Precious Times' highlights how fleeting those moments we share with loved ones and it reminds us how even 'boring' times form the beautiful tapestry of life.

And when the life of our loved one finally concludes, what has been experienced is unique to each and every one of us.

"But the life I had when you were here,

Was more than good enough ..."

UNIQUE AND PRECIOUS TIMES

Despite the bitter sting of grief,
I try to smile through the tears.
And reflect upon those bygone times,
We enjoyed throughout the years.

Remembering fun times at the seaside,
Then complaining at household chores.
And days which were neither bad nor good,
But were mine, as they were yours.

But now, everywhere that I look,
And everything my eyes can see.
Reminds me so much of all we shared,
And I think we'd both agree ...

... That life was often far from perfect,
In all honesty it could be tough.
But the life I had when you were here,
Was more than good enough.

Time goes by so very fast,
And when the final second chimes,
Memories are all that are left behind.
Of uniquely precious times.

© Hazel Prosser 2023

DEAR GRIEF ... YOU WILL NOT WIN!

Anger often accompanies grief. For me personally, losing my parents generated a great deal of anger which I initially directed towards myself. I felt inadequate, wondering if I could have done more. As time went on this anger became overwhelming and I blamed the universe for taking them away.

When I lost George, I accepted an invitation to visit Australia, believing that I would be able to escape from my all-encompassing grief. But I couldn't. The anger I felt at his loss could not be outrun.

Similarly, when Hugo passed right in the middle of the pandemic I could barely contain my anger. Though I understood what needed to happen and why, not being able to be with him during his final minutes was heart-wrenching. I couldn't bear for anyone to offer words of solace.

Joining a pet loss support group marked the beginning of my healing journey. I learned to compartmentalise my anger and express my emotions (through writing, for example) rather than allowing these to consume me. ' Dear Grief' was one of the poems I wrote to create a platform for communicating with my grief, which has helped me to reflect. I now understand my anger, that it has its place, and whilst it has not been easy, I recognise it for what it is. Part of the healing process.

As the late great Queen Elizabeth II once said: *"Grief is the price we pay for love."*

DEAR GRIEF ..... YOU WILL NOT WIN!

Why must you visit, and pierce my heart?
When my soul's engulfed in pain,
My eyes stinging through bitter tears,
Yet, an inner strength I must sustain.

You mock me at my lowest ebb,
When death took the one, I love,
Such turmoil in each day and night,
But there's a Guardian Angel up above.

You see, you may be such a bitter foe,
But you will never win this war,
When two souls are forever tied,
You'll soon be shown the door.

So do your worst, I'll cry those tears,
Then like the Winter's curse,
Begone and leave my heart to heal,
Because memories will reimburse.

They will move the clouds and clear my mind,
Radiance will lift my soul.
In your absence, joy and warmth,
Will fill that gaping hole.

With guidance from the one I loved,
I know I'll see a sign.
That I was theirs for all eternity,
And they, indeed were mine.

Grief - You are the price we pay for love,
Momentarily I'll let you in,
But you cannot steal invisible ties,
Life may end, but love will win!

© Hazel Prosser 2022

I KNOW YOU CAN STILL HEAR ME

The best 'overview' I can give of this poem, is to describe it as a 'thank you' letter.

As a child after every Christmas and Birthday, my brother and I would sit at the Dining Room table under our Mother's guidance, individually writing 'thank you' letters for presents received. This tradition I still carry on today - even if it is by way of e-mail.

By far the most precious and priceless gifts in my life are my animals. When I talk to those no longer at my side, (either out loud or just in my head) I genuinely believe they hear me and send 'signs' as affirmations. These signs strengthen my belief of an invisible connection – of a friendship for life and beyond.

I KNOW YOU CAN STILL HEAR ME

In life we were inseparable,
And still the same is true.
My heart will forever carry,
The love I have for you.

I recognise how blessed I was,
Cherished with friendship such as yours.
Big gentle eyes, plush velvet coat,
Such precious little paws.

"I know you can still hear me".
I whisper through gulps and tears.
My heart and soul are shattered,
As I reflect on all the years.

When the angels softly spoke,
And called you to their home.
They didn't seem to comprehend,
I'd be bereft and all alone.

Yet, I know you rest so peacefully,
Bathed in celestial guiding light.
And you'll always be right by my side,
Though hidden from my sight.

Thanks to you my little one,
From the bottom of my heart.
I know that when we meet once more,
Never shall we part.

© Hazel Prosser 2022

NATURE'S INVITATION

There have been times when I struggled to leave my house after going through a loss. One day, though, even as my emotions urged me to stay within my comfort zone, I decided to make a deliberate effort and go for a walk along the canal.

The weather was absolutely perfect. The sky was a beautiful shade of azure blue adorned with fluffy white clouds, and the birds were happily chirping in the trees. The gentle breeze caused a rustling in the branches and the flowers swayed gracefully in answer.

As I walked alongside the tranquil water, occasionally seeing a narrowboat pass by, a sense of peace and serenity washed over me. Raw emotions that had clamoured for me to stay inside, began to feel soothed as Mother Nature delivered her tonic.

Such was the effect on me that it felt only right to dictate a few words into my phone as I continued my walk. I knew the real world would return soon enough, but in that moment, I was loved and supported in a way I could only describe through the words of this poem.

NATURE'S INVITATION

When the heart is heavy,
And the eyes are tear-filled pools.
Encased by the ache in your heart,
Memories glisten like jewels

The outside world,
Seems to bustle and trill.
But in the isolation of grief,
Life has become unrecognisably still.

With a glance outside,
You see Mother Nature open her hand
By accepting her invitation
Together you stand.

Flowers acknowledge your presence,
As they wave gently in the breeze.
Crackling branches noisily,
Beckon a welcome from trees

Sunshine beats down so warmly,
There's a blue sky up above.
Gradually your spirit is lifted,
As you're surrounded by love

Slowly, a feather drifts downwards,
A sign so sparkling and white.
Bringing much needed reassurance,
Your loved one is only gone from your sight.

© Hazel Prosser 2023

THE FEATHER IN THE WOODS

This poem is a amalgamation of my love of nature and animals. As I walk in nature I always reflect and will often see signs that I know are my cats, telling me they're okay.

'The Feather in the Woods' is my way of remembering George and Hugo, my British Shorthairs who I still miss every day. It is also a reminder of Oliver and Oscar, my gorgeous Blue-Point Persians who I was blessed to have in my life, before George and Hugo.

When I write as I spend time in nature and allow my imagination to flow, I am able to draw on so many emotions. This poem, I believe, is not only a timeless tribute but also a precis of life as we each continue our journey.

THE FEATHER IN THE WOODS

Wondrous is my peaceful walk,
Through a glade that's evergreen.
Remembering you with fondness
Before emotions intervene.

The walk continues until I know,
My head can take no more,
Images roll down my face,
And become fiery tears galore.

Ahead I see a little bench,
Ancient and worse for wear,
It still provides some respite though,
From inescapable despair.

I take a moment to look around,
At scenery undisturbed,
But in that moment I see something new
Confirming you have heard.

You're listening to my inner thoughts,
Oh, beautiful friend of mine,
My spirit lifts, and my heart it bursts,
Seeing a special sign.

A tiny feather, white as snow,
Appears at my feet,
I reach down to pick it up,
From my rickety little seat.

The feather skips as if it wants,
To have a bit of fun,
I follow it with curiosity,
Seeing it glistening in the sun.

It stops once more, I try again,
To take it from the land.
This time, it rises of its own accord,
And settles in my hand.

This is you; I know for sure,
You always brought me joy,
You saw light where there was dark,
My precious little boy.

You're telling me that you're just fine,
In your new world up above,
The sparkling sign I'll keep with me,
As your heavenly gift of love.

© Hazel Prosser 2020

CANDLELIGHT REFLECTIONS

Writing 'Candlelight Reflections' was not intentional! In fact, it was written on a day where the weather outside was a typical one for April in the UK, (sunshine and showers in quick succession).

It happened to be one of those days where I didn't really know what to do, so as shadows were cast across my living room I lit a candle, one with a scent I love, and sat in my favourite armchair trying to decide how to spend the time productively.

As I relaxed, I found my eyes closing and memories playing in my mind's eye. As I remembered some I have loved and lost, tears began to fall accompanied by a weight of sadness, despite the purring cat resting on my lap.

Suddenly I became aware that the candle scent was getting stronger, so I opened my eyes to check it was okay. As soon as I focused, I saw wax falling from the top to the bottom, their shapes bearing an uncanny resemblance to the tears that had fallen from my eyes. It felt as if the candle was crying too, echoing my emotions so I began to dictate a few words into my phone. Words that would go on to become this poem.

CANDLELIGHT REFLECTIONS

The evening is so peaceful,
Though I hear the clock ticking merrily.
As I muse in quiet reflection,
Waves of emotion wash over me.

Adding some ambience to the silence,
I light the fragrant candle in the jar.
Seeing the flame ignite and flicker,
I truly wonder where you are.

Settling back into my comfy chair,
Eyes closed; yet seeing what's in my mind's eye.
All the images of our together times,
Replay so clearly and I begin to cry.

The tears cannot wash out those pictures,
In fact, they make the colour brighter.
If I'd only known then, what I know now,
I'd have hugged you so much tighter.

Through my tears which are hotly pouring,
I can't help but smile at all we shared.
Our hopes and dreams, and fears and worries,
Yet never was I prepared.

To live a life without you,
To answer questions for myself.
The scent from the candle fills the room,
My eyes open and look towards the shelf.

The melting wax has caused tear shaped patterns,
To trickle down the jar.
Somehow I feel you're hearing me,
And listening from afar.

As my eyes close once more,
Falling tears have dried upon my cheek.
I want you, my dear departed one,
To embrace these words, I speak.

You trod the ground, for the life I now live,
And for each granted and new tomorrow.
Your legacy I'll carry like the Olympic torch,
In your memory and honour I'll follow.

The little flame on the candle,
Has almost burnt right to its core.
But alight within my heart, is an eternal flame,
Until we can be together once more

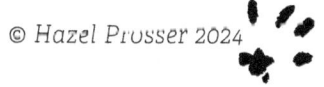

© Hazel Prosser 2024

LITTLE ROBIN

As I have mentioned in other overviews, I have a deep appreciation for spiritual 'signs' and hold a strong belief that our departed loved ones send them to reassure us they have found peace in the afterlife. I see these signs as gentle nudges which can help us navigate through our grief and to continue with our lives.

I have been fortunate to receive various signs, such as feathers and butterflies and even a random melody played on my 'Alexa', which coincided with Hugo's passing. The most prevalent of them all, though, is the charming little robin.

The European Robin is a delightful bird, with a rotund, cheerful demeanour and a vibrant red breast. Though often associated with Christmas, this bird can be seen all year round and never fails to bring a smile to my face.

Shortly after losing George in September 2009, I found myself in the back garden with tears streaming down my face. Suddenly I heard the most beautiful sound causing me to pause. A sweet little robin had landed on the fence and was watching me as it chirped, swaying its little head from side to side. As I listened, a stillness came over me and I wondered if this was a messenger from the unseen world. From George.

Later, the words for this poem formed, whispered from my soul during that beautiful moment in the garden. I urge you to look out for signs and remain open to their meaning, because love is eternal and survives even death.

LITTLE ROBIN

Oh! Little robin on the tree,
My unique, exquisite sign.
A messenger from a world unseen,
Where the heart and soul entwine.

Chirping so merrily from the branch,
Flaunting your bright red breast of love.
I know you've come to illustrate,
The beauty of a paradise up above.

You've been asked to pay this visit,
Which reassures me that my loved one is at peace.
And yet, is still around me night and day,
In the hope that my grief will cease.

Upon your wing, please carry,
My eternal love and pride.
To the devoted pet I miss so much,
Who is absent from my side.

Little robin I know your wings are strong,
As you gracefully soar into the skies.
Returning to the One who meant the most,
Tenderly proving that love never dies.

© Hazel Prosser 2022

MOON GAZING HARE

Have you ever seen a Hare?

Despite being one of the UK's most adorable wild animals, (and notwithstanding the fact I live in a village), until a couple of years ago, I had never seen one.

Of course, as is always the way, when, finally I did see one, I was driving home from work, and it took me a while to realise that what I had just passed was more than simply a 'big rabbit'.

Since then, I've seen others. They amuse me. Independent, long and gangly, big, oversized ears and huge, great feet - kind of describes me as a teenager!

In my back garden at home, I have a couple of Moon Gazing Hare ornaments – one of them holds the moon in its paws and has a mystical quality. I have always believed that animals can see into another dimension, and, given that the hare has such beautiful eyes and big ears, I love the idea of them being our conduit. Of being able to see and hear those we miss most. Perhaps even becoming our spirit guides.

In ancient times, hares were believed to be sacred animals with connections to the afterlife which ties in nicely with my own thoughts, so I decided to put all of this together and create one wondrous poem - The Moon Gazing Hare.

The thought that these animals unite my world with the next, gives me great comfort.

MOON GAZING HARE

Moon Gazing Hare, what is it you see,
As you stare up at the ebony skies?
Peppered with stars, glistening and bright,
Entrancing your gentle brown eyes.

Moon Gazing Hare, with your ears so long,
Listening to words spoken from a world unseen.
Loved ones who rest in eternal glory,
Ask that you now intervene.

Moon Gazing Hare, as you stamp your big paws,
Acknowledging all you are told.
I see how you jump, conveying messages of peace,
Which help my heart to be eased and consoled.

Moon Gazing Hare, will you send all my love,
Back to those from whom you can hear.
And tell them how they were one in a million,
Devoted, loyal, true and sincere.

Moon Gazing Hare, with your shimmering fur,
Your presence soothes all the tears that I cry.
A Guardian Angel sent to watch over me,
To reassure, I've only said farewell ... Not goodbye.

© Hazel Prosser 2023

SECTION FIVE

Poetry for
FRIENDS AND EMPLOYERS

GROUNDING THOUGHTS

Writing 'Grounding Thoughts' was a unique experience for me. Instead of expressing my personal emotions directly, I crafted a mythical tale that explores how grief can manifest in our imaginations. I believe that escapism can be so beneficial, after all, the world around us offers countless wonders to divert our attention.

Before I began writing poetry in my current style, I used to create similes which allowed me to compare my grief to entirely different scenarios. With 'Grounding Thoughts', my intention was to blend elements from the outside, the gifts of Mother Nature and spiritual signs, along with exercise, emotions and grounding - all then connected to the profound love we hold for those we miss.

The first time I shared this writing, a friend told me that she could vividly imagine the scene and even felt she could 'smell' the air. I knew then that by linking my personal grief to nature, this poem would bring solace and comfort.

Allow yourself a precious moment with a cuppa as you read these words and, if you can, truly absorb and feel their message.

(Just a quick note: In this context, 'grounding' can also be referred to as 'earthing' which involves finding ways to connect ourselves with the earth - hence walking in bare feet and needing to put my shoes back on!)

GROUNDING THOUGHTS

Morning eclipses the darkness of night,
Birds sing a merry dawn chorus through trees.
A heady elixir of sparkling cool air,
Is perfumed with honey and nectar from bees.

The alchemy of thoughts in my mind,
Nature's cocktail of scents I inhale.
Pausing to absorb and ingest all I can,
Ensuring the goodness of life will prevail.

Without hesitation, I remove the shoes that I wear,
Planting my feet deep into soft, earthy ground.
With thoughts of you, my eyes ascend to the sky,
I feel connected, in tune and spellbound.

For you still to be here, my heart yearns,
My eyes bubble and leak at this thought.
I take a deep breath to the core of my lungs,
And slowly recalling all that you taught.

The ground that I stand on connects us,
Our worlds conjoin, uniting as one.
I feel sunshine's invigorating rays on my face,
As though a new journey has suddenly begun.

The rain breaks its way through the sunlight,
Pounding a beat on the earth where I stand.
It's now that I sense you're around me,
As a rainbow wraps the sky with a colourful band.

Somehow my tears hook a smile from my lips,
A confetti of emotions cascade and appear.
From nowhere the prettiest white butterfly,
A sign your presence is unquestionably near.

A joy in my heart gets me walking,
Towards a little bench so rickety and worn.
Seated I shake off the soil and put my shoes on
Feeling uplifted and somehow reborn

The butterfly follows me for a short while longer,
Before it settles on the back of my hand.
Stretching its wings so perfectly outwards,
As though confirming that I do understand.

I nod and I thank it so graciously,
Wishing it god speed for the journey above.
Not ever can our spirits be parted,
We are eternally linked with one love.

© Hazel Prosser 2022

THE GRIEVING EMPLOYEE

I have been employed in one capacity or another for well over 30 years. In that time, not only have I been bereaved of my own adored animals, but I have supported work colleagues who have faced a similar situation. In the majority of cases, despite trying to deal with the overwhelming emotions associated with pet loss, employees are generally expected to return to work almost immediately.

One vivid recollection from some 25 years ago was when I was working as an estate agent. I recall how a colleague, upon arrival, put her bag on her desk and then promptly burst into tears. Of course, I, along with another colleague asked if we could help, and were told that her elderly dog was due to be euthanised that day.

The manager, on hearing the woman's tears, came over to see "what the fuss was about" and when enlightened, brusquely told her this was "absolutely no excuse" for being late into work (she was no more than quarter-of-an-hour late). He then continued his objectionable behaviour by stating, "it wasn't like it was a person". "A dog is just a dog," he said, "There will always be others!".

When this colleague returned to work after lunch, she was incredibly upset and of course struggled to be productive, but this didn't make any impression on the manager who poured scorn over her 'childish' tears. When I took him to task for his insensitivity, he reiterated his instruction that I was not to get involved and to get on with my own work.

Sadly, though we have come a long way, even today situations such as these are not unusual and it is my greatest hope through the medium of this book that employers can become more educated about what pet loss can mean. If an employee has been bereaved of an animal, I genuinely feel they should be offered compassion, not ridiculed or forced to suppress grief. This, in my experience, only compounds the grief which will often lead to longer absences from work.

There is now bespoke help for those grieving pet loss and I have included some helpful links at the end of the book. If, as an employer, you are able to help your employee feel supported and looked after during these times, then it is only natural for them to become your greatest asset and to remain loyal - perhaps when you need them the most.

It costs nothing to offer support, and to console an employee or colleague bereaved of a pet.

THE GRIEVING EMPLOYEE

My employer doesn't understand,
The pain that's gnawing deep inside.
They don't see or hear the 'real me',
Let alone, notice infinite tears I have cried.

Someone told them, I've "Lost a pet",
Describing a chattel nothing more.
Without any comprehension whatsoever,
My feelings are as painful as they are raw.

In passing, I hear "By the way, I'm sorry,"
Merged with "How old was your pet."
Quickly dismissing my pained expression,
Because at work, I'm supposed to "just forget"!

Pet loss cannot be branded,
Inconsequential and weak.
Just because one grieves for something,
That had fur, wool, hair, or even feathers and beak!

Employers I impress upon you,
Should you have staff bereaved of their pet.
Did you know there are pet loss advisors,
Who offer a confidential and dedicated outlet?

Please talk to your employee,
About the animal that they grieve.
Validate how they are feeling,
Give them hope to believe …

That they are still very much needed,
A significant part of your team.
That you appreciate they will struggle,
When emotions intervene.

Once the heartache subsides,
And grief detaches its powerful greed.
Your employee will surely remember,
How they were supported, during their 'hour of need'.

© Hazel Prosser 2023

DEAR FRIEND, DON'T FORSAKE ME NOW
(When Grief Hurts a Friendship)

During a period of grief, I also lost a friendship. One that had until then, endured the test of time. The result was a sense of multiplied mourning.

It happened in 2003 following the passing of my Dad. A long-time friend from my school days made a hurtful remark, telling me that I was 'too maudlin' and because of this, they felt unable to continue our friendship. Not only did that moment mark the end of what I had considered to be a strong bond, it also left me feeling angry and confused. I had been there for them when they had experienced loss, so what was different when I was the one in need? This, though, led me to be more guarded of my actions and reactions after I lost Mum and I started to wonder if I was somehow at fault. Was I placing unreasonable expectations on my friends? Was my grief negatively impacting them? I am still plagued by these concerns, today.

What I have come to understand, however, is that grief follows its own unique timeline making it challenging for others to consistently provide support. Often, individuals are dealing with their own personal struggles which may limit their capacity to empathise and offer care. I believe it's crucial, then, to strike a balance between giving and receiving in a friendship, and to recognise that if a friend becomes distant, it may not be because of *your* grief, but because their own situation is currently too overwhelming.

DEAR FRIEND, DON'T FORSAKE ME NOW
(When Grief Hurts a Friendship)

You say I'm good with words,
And whilst this may be true.
What I write today,
Is done with honesty for you.

I know in recent times,
Upon your strength I've lent.
Oh, grief has made me selfish,
Of this I do lament.

My friend just know I realise,
You have the biggest heart.
Whilst blinded by emotions,
Our friendship began to split apart.

Grief has so many fathoms,
Sometimes appearing cold and raw.
And it's been the thief of the real me,
Right to the very core.

It pushes over boundaries,
And causes huge mistakes.
Whilst nobody is perfect,
Friendships it forsakes.

You have offered so much guidance,
With incredible clarity.
This has given me the impetus,
To begin adjusting to a new normality.

With your help, my soul feels light,
Where once it was so grey.
I'm pushing through the nemesis,
And moving it away.

The laughter and the humour,
Shared mutually in the past.
Will return as strong as ever,
For friendships are made to last.

So smile my friend and thank you,
You can be so very proud.
You've embroidered threads of silver,
Into a dark and intense cloud.

Friendships, they are heaven sent,
And truly meant to be.
So with thanks and love and kindness,
Here's to the future – our epiphany.

© Hazel Prosser 2023

SECTION SIX

BESPOKE Poetry

Occasionally, my friends request poems for their pets, or I may write one for them. 'Dear Skye' was a specific request whilst 'Chosen' was a poem I elected to write. Cheryl and Kenda, Skye and Stella's owners, have kindly allowed me to include these poems here.

The loss of a pet can leave us feeling empty but it's comforting to know that we are not alone. As you read these poems I hope you can relate not only with the pets, but also with their bereaved owners.

DEAR SKYE

"Hazel, would you consider writing a poem for Skye?" Cheryl asked.

I was flabbergasted. How could I possibly write a poem for someone else? What if I said the wrong thing? What if I caused further upset?

Cheryl and I met through the Healing Solutions for Pet Loss group run by Kenda Summers on Facebook. Though we live in different countries, we've formed a connection and chat often, yet to be asked to capture Skye, Cheryl's beloved Border Collie who had recently passed, felt overwhelming. Before this, I had only ever written for my own healing journey.

Cheryl was insistent, though, and reassured me that no matter what, she would be grateful. She just wanted a way to remember Skye and couldn't think of anything more perfect than a poem.

My initial concern was how to capture Skye in a way that did her and Cheryl's love justice, so I asked Cheryl to provide me with everything she could remember about Skye, from the day she brought her home. Using these memories and anecdotes I slowly built a picture of Skye and after a time, was able to write the following poem.

When it was finished, I shared it nervously and was blown away when Cheryl told me that not only did she love it, but that she would be framing it on her wall - something to read every day to remind her of her companion.

> *Run free at Rainbow Bridge, beautiful Skye; you were a joy to write about and a very special friend.*

('Dear Skye' is published here with kind permission of Cheryl Garcia)

DEAR SKYE

The first day that I met you,
I saw a pup so beautiful, smart and fun.
A sparkling glint adorned amber eyes,
My heart knew you were the one.

Running my fingers through your spangled coat,
Caressing velvet ears,
Heaven sent by angels,
To be my soulmate through the years.

Mischievously searching through my purse,
You grabbed my glasses case!
I laughed so hard until I cried,
In hot pursuit your siblings soon gave chase!

Scooping you up into my arms,
My face awash with loving kisses,
Though once at home you had to learn.
A teased Siamese cat responds with hisses!

I'd describe your heart as solid gold,
Your intelligence shone so bright.
You loved your walks, your toys, your treats,
And challenging the hose to a water fight!

Our days turned into months, then years,
Memories embroidered them all,
We'd roam for miles together,
Never forgetting your favourite ball!.

With pride you'd show off all your tricks,
Which I taught you with so much ease,
Including singing on command,
I was the audience you loved to please!

Rewarding you with little treats,
Such as a trip to 'Starbucks' coffee shop.
"Would you like a 'Puppuccino' Skye?"
Straight into the car you'd hop!

Momentarily cream clung to your whiskered face,
But your tongue swept it all away,
You looked at me as if to say,
"Mommy, can we do this every day?!"

Life wasn't always easy,
It brought many struggles too,
A comforting paw upon my knee,
Turned all grey skies to blue.

Our time together passed too quickly,
  You taught me what love meant,
  Every moment living life with you,
    Was a time in life well spent.

My friend, my confidante, my heart and soul,
      Each day was such a gift,
    Sadly, the day arrived far too soon,
When the angels called on your soul to lift.

    The day you eternally fell asleep,
      My heart was in such pain,
    But I know that when the time is right,
        We will walk together again.

You were certainly one in a million,
  Unique and special to me,
  My friend, my world, my beautiful girl,
  Our souls entwined eternally.

In Memory of Skye

CHOSEN

Although having good intentions for friends is admirable, there are times when they can be misunderstood - especially during moments of grief. This is something that always concerns me when it comes to writing bespoke pieces.

'Chosen', was initially intended for Kenda Summers and her husband Dr Jim Wand, as a memorial of their beautiful dog, Stella. When Kenda had lost Stella, she created a pet loss group called, 'Healing Solutions for Pet Loss', which became a source of comfort and healing for me, particularly when I lost Hugo.

In 2021, having become close to Kenda and Jim via this group, I learned the devastating news that Jim had been diagnosed with a terminal health condition. Given all that they had done for me, I knew I wanted to express my thoughts and gratitude, but I didn't know how to do so - especially as they lived in the USA. Then, in late November of 2021, it came to me. I realised that the perfect way to show both Kenda and Jim how much they meant to me was to write, and thus, 'Chosen' was born.

It was so difficult to know what to write - I kept adding and then deleting, adding and then deleting, so afraid of overstepping boundaries or causing undue upset. Finally, just before Christmas Eve of the same year, 'Chosen' was ready and I gathered to courage to send it to Kenda. Her response was simple. *"This is so incredibly beautiful!"*

On hearing those words, my fears melted away. Though it was unexpected, Kenda's response was so sincere that I knew I'd been right to push through those nagging doubts.

('Chosen' is published here with kind permission of Kenda Summers)

CHOSEN

(In Loving Memory of 'Stella – The Golden Entrancer')

The guardian angels looked to earth,
And together they did decide.
We need to send our chosen one,
To be a human companion and guide.

They scoured their celestial garden,
To find a spirit calm and wise.
One who'd graced the earth before,
And could be sent down in disguise.

They knew the perfect little soul,
Would be the teacher they would lend.
But more than this a confidante,
Mentor and best friend.

The eternal beaming sunshine,
Shone upon illustrious golden fur.
An archangel placed his hands on it,
Smiled and said "This is her."

Kneeling at her side,
He whispered softly in her ear.
Gentle words she understood,
With instructions that were clear.

For a short duration you are lent,
To the people you see below.
Our chosen one, this is your time,
To teach them all you know.

Thereafter a little pup was born,
Her mission understood.
She would be an entertainer,
Proud, beautiful, and good.

For two whole years she travelled,
Bringing laughter and smiles galore.
She knew her earthly time was short,
With the humans she did adore.

Looking around and with a bark,
Enlightened those so near.
Though I'll soon depart, I will live on,
And soothe every glistening tear.

My duty is for those I love,
To continue my role.
To reach out to others in their sorrow,
And heal their grieving soul.

And on the day, she did depart,
As her spirit rose and flew.
An archangel greeted her,
Exclaiming "We're all so very proud of you!"

You were given an exceptionally special task,
  Which you've carried out with zeal.
In your honour, your work lives on,
  As you watch others heal.

Then he patted her on the head,
  And she stared right up at him.
She was told she'd walk at the angel's side,
  But stay close to Kenda and Jim.

They will forever need you,
  To be their earth angel for all time.
To show them you have never left,
  You'll send many a frequent sign.

And so, with thanks to Stella,
  And the work she did so grand.
She's healing us through our grief and pain,
  And helping us understand.

When our beloved pets do transcend,
  To a realm beyond our sight.
    They remain forever in our hearts,
      Through love's eternal light.

ABOUT THE AUTHOR

Born in the Royal town of Sutton Coldfield, England, Hazel learned from a young age, how devastating grief could be. With parents considered 'older' when she was born, it was inevitable that loss would become an integral part of her life.

As a three-month old baby, the family sadly lost their beloved miniature poodle, Charlotte, and though Hazel is too young to remember Charlotte, her mother would talk about the little dog often. Hazel is convinced that her mother never truly got over this loss, often telling Hazel how long it had taken her to recover from the grief.

At the age of four and a half, Hazel was forced to spend an extended period away from her parents when her mother was hospitalised for several weeks ahead of the birth of her younger brother. Cared for by relatives, Hazel nevertheless found the separation difficult, especially when it coincided with her father being away on jury service.

Animals came and went throughout Hazel's life and it is in their memory she has created the photo spread in the centre of this book. As she references in many of her poems, Hazel has always felt safe and loved by animals who have been constant companions during a life which hasn't always been easy.

Writing became a way for Hazel to express her emotions, and poetry her method of choice. She would spend hours writing everything she was feeling into flowing verses which she would then safely tuck away, never intending her words to be read by anyone else. Life, though, as it so often does, presented Hazel with an opportunity to share some of her poetry - specifically those around pet loss and grief - and the rest, as they say, is history.

Whispering to your Heart is a culmination of a lifetime of work and the beginning of a dream that Hazel still can't believe is real.

SECTION SEVEN

HELPFUL RESOURCES

For additional support, I've included a list of contacts that may be beneficial. Please note: I am not endorsing any of these organisations, simply providing them as a starting point for your journey of healing.

Though most of the organisations listed are UK based, similar services are available worldwide. A quick internet search should help you find some that may be more specific to your need or location.

For Pet Loss

- **BLUE CROSS**
  www.bluecross.org.uk/pet-bereavement-and-pet-loss
  Email: pbssmail@bluecross.org.uk
  Telephone: 0800 096 6606

- **CATS PROTECTION (PAWS TO LISTEN)**
  www.cats.org.uk/what-we-do/grief/advice
  Telephone: 0800 024 9494

- **DIGNIPETS**
  Veterinary in-home hospice and end of life care for pets.
  www.dignipets.co.uk
  Email: enquiries@dignipets.co.uk
  Telephone: 0333 320 8731

- **THE BRITISH HORSE SOCIETY (FRIENDS AT THE END)**
  www.bhs.org.uk/horse-care-and-welfare/health-care-management/euthanasia/friends-at-the-end/
  Email: welfare@bhs.org.uk
  Telephone: 02476 840517

- **PET SORROW**
  www.petsorrow.com

  Pet Sorrow is a pet loss website owned, run and managed by Author, Hypnotist and NLP Practitioner Kenda Summers. A true devoted animal lover, Kenda has owned many different animals during her lifetime, including dogs, cats and horses. Her book entitled *Healing Solutions for Pet Loss – Goodbye is Not Forever* is not just a story but a companion guide for those suffering the loss of a pet and is full of useful information. Accompanying her website, there is the Facebook group entitled *'Healing Solutions for Pet Loss'*.

- **THE RALPH SITE**

  www.theralphsite.com

  The Ralph site was set up by vet Shailen Jasani (MA VetMB MRCVS DipACVECC) in July 2011 after the loss of his beloved cat, Ralph, following a motor vehicle accident in November 2010. The site is dedicated to all the animals that have touched and continue to touch the hearts of so many people.

For Other Loss

- **SAMARITANS**

  www.samaritans.org

  Telephone: 116 123

- **THE LIGHTHOUSE CLUB CHARITY (for construction workers)**

  www.lighthouseclub.org

  Telephone (UK): 0345 605 1956

  Telephone (ROI): 1800 939 122

- **CRUSE BEREAVEMENT SUPPORT**

  www.cruse.org.uk

  Telephone: 0808 8081677

THE WHISPERING JOURNAL
A Place For My Thoughts

www.ingramcontent.com/pod-product-compliance
Lightning Source LLC
Chambersburg PA
CBHW041306110526
44590CB00028B/4260